GREEN BELT
WORD SEARCH
PUZZLES

PATRICK BLINDAUER ▶

A G (V E R M E E R) O O D
(R E M B R A N D T) P A I
N H V A   H T I N
G C T   MARTIAL ARTS Word Search   H A S
I I   B L
N Y   N E
A   E I
I L   I I
L A   R I
G M E   E R
I E P K   NOT-SO-EASY   M E L O
D C O L M H C N U M E T
O P L E D E A E A G A H

80 PUZZLES

PUZZLE
WRIGHT
PRESS

New York

**PUZZLE
WRIGHT
PRESS**

New York

An Imprint of Sterling Publishing
1166 Avenue of the Americas
New York, NY 10036

© 2015 by Patrick Blindauer

ISBN 978-1-4549-1212-5

Distributed in Canada by Sterling Publishing
c/o Canadian Manda Group, 664 Annette Street
Toronto, Ontario, Canada M6S 2C8
Distributed in the United Kingdom by GMC Distribution Services
Castle Place, 166 High Street, Lewes, East Sussex, England BN7 1XU
Distributed in Australia by Capricorn Link (Australia) Pty. Ltd.
P.O. Box 704, Windsor, NSW 2756, Australia

For information about custom editions, special sales, and premium
and corporate purchases, please contact Sterling Special Sales
at 800-805-5489 or specialsales@sterlingpublishing.com.

Manufactured in Canada

2 4 6 8 10 9 7 5 3 1

www.puzzlewright.com

Contents

Introduction

Hello there, wacky word-searchers! Welcome to "Green Belt Word Search Puzzles," the second in a four-part series of word search books designed to increase your word-searching prowess through a regimen of increasingly difficult puzzles. Here the word lists are a little trickier than they were in "White Belt Word Search Puzzles," with more unfamiliar topics and unusual spellings of esoteric people, places, and things. There are even a few puzzles at the end of the book that will give you a sense of what the third book in the series has in store.

In case word searches are new to you, let me break down the basics: You will be presented with a list of answers and a grid of letters, and it's up to you to find every answer hidden somewhere in the grid. The answers in this book will always be in a straight line and could be traveling in any one of eight possible directions (forward to the right, backward to the left, up, down, diagonally up and to the left, diagonally up and to the right, diagonally down and to the left, or diagonally down and to the right).

As you find each answer word or phrase, you should mark it in the grid somehow (and mark it off the list, as well). Lots of people like to mark their answers in the grid by making a giant loop, but for this book I recommend circling the letters individually, drawing a line through your answer, or using a highlighter. This will make it easier to read the final message at the end. Oh, didn't I tell you? The leftover letters spell out a quote that relates to the theme of the puzzle. Just read the unused letters from left to right, row by row, starting at the top. The source of the quote is either in the leftovers or the introductory text, and all the quotes can be found with the answers starting on page 169.

Something else that may help you is the fact that all of the answers in each puzzle are fully interlocked. That is, there are no isolated islands of words. So don't ignore letters just because you've used them already. Things that you can and should ignore are punctuation, diacritcal markings, and anything that's in brackets.

A few words of thanks to the people who made this book possible: to my parents, Wayne and Sharon, for encouraging my creativity and for instilling a lifelong love of language; to my wife, Rebecca, for all of her love and assistance on this book; to Puzzlewright Press editors Peter Gordon and Francis Heaney for their expertise and patience; and to Dan Feyer for his astute testing.

If you enjoy these puzzles, be sure to check out the other books in the series: "White Belt Word Search Puzzles," "Brown Belt Word Search Puzzles," and "Black Belt Word Search Puzzles." If you like crosswords, look for some of my other books or visit my website, where I post monthly crosswords and host crossword contests. Happy solving!

—Patrick Blindauer
www.patrickblindauer.com

Puzzles

1. STATE OF THE ART

Find all the painters hiding in the grid. The leftover letters spell a quote by Hedy Lamarr.

BACON
BASQUIAT
BOTTICELLI
CARAVAGGIO
CÉZANNE
DALÍ
DEGAS
GAUGUIN
GOYA
JOHNS
KAHLO
KANDINSKY
KLEE
KLIMT
[DE] KOONING
MAGRITTE
MALEVICH
MANET

MATISSE
MODIGLIANI
MONET
MUNCH
PICASSO
PISSARRO
POLLOCK
RAPHAEL
REMBRANDT
RENOIR
ROTHKO
RUBENS
SEURAT
TITIAN
VAN GOGH
VERMEER
WARHOL

```
A G V E R M E E R O O D
R E M B R A N D T P A I
N H V A N G O G H T I N
G C T O T R N M E H A S
I I A T A I U Q S A B L
N V W A U T S N H O J N
A E Y G E T S S T B A E
I L U N E E N T E I L I
L A A K E A I R T F R I
G M E N D C I I T K E R
I E P K E S T O M E L O
D C O L M H C N U M E T
O P L E D E A E A G A H
M I K E Z Y B R N N H K
W Y G A O S S A C I P O
C A N G N K O M C N A R
S N R E A D C F O O R R
E R B H K V I O T O N A
U U S L O A A N L K I S
R A I N D L H R S L I S
A M N S P I R L A K O I
T E N O M E S D O C Y P
```

Answer on page 170.

2. TONGUE-TIED

Find all the languages hiding in the grid. The leftover letters spell a quote by George Bernard Shaw.

ARABIC	ORIYA
BENGALI	PASHTO
CZECH	PERSIAN
DUTCH	POLISH
ENGLISH	PORTUGUESE
FRENCH	PUNJABI
GERMAN	RUSSIAN
GREEK	SPANISH
HAKKA	SUNDANESE
HAUSA	SWAHILI
HINDI	TAGALOG
HUNGARIAN	TAMIL
INDONESIAN	TELUGU
ITALIAN	THAI
KANNADA	TURKISH
KOREAN	URDU
MALAGASY	VIETNAMESE
MANDARIN	XIANG
MARATHI	ZULU
MIN NAN	

```
E S N G L S W A H I L I
N P P U N J A B I P H A
N A D A N D E A E T M O
E N N R I N C R A A T A
R I E N G L S R T H W O
C S P A I I A N S C E O
U H L O A M N A T E S T
R I S N R A P M E Z E I
U E D I F T S R L C N S
R E Y N K R U E U P A G
D Z A S I R E G G R D R
U A U T A H U N U E N E
T G O L A G A T C E U E
C D B K U I A Y Y H S K
H I K T X K N L I N O E
S A B H M A N D A R I N
I E S A I N A I E M O G
L M E S R N L A L A N L
O E S E M A N T E I V I
P U G U T D H A U S A S
R N A I R A G N U H A H
G E N A I S E N O D N I
```

3. "THE HUNGER GAMES"

Find all the character names hiding in the grid.
The leftover letters spell a quote
spoken by Peeta in the novel.

ANNIE	JOHANNA
BEETEE	KATNISS
CAESAR	MAGS
CASHMERE	MARVEL
CINNA	OCTAVIA
CLOVE	PEETA MELLARK
CRESSIDA	PLUTARCH
ENOBARIA	HEAVENSBEE
FINNICK	POLLUX
FLAVIUS	PRIMROSE
FOXFACE	RUE
GALE HAWTHORNE	SENECA CRANE
GLIMMER	THRESH
GLOSS	TIGRIS
GREASY SAE	TITUS
HAYMITCH	WIRESS
ABERNATHY	

```
O N F I N N I C K L G E
Y I M A R V E L K A R E
E E E C A F X O F I E B
P W I S S H I V Y R A S
X U L L O P N E H A S N
G I E S I R G I T B Y E
K C O R U L M T A O S V
D R G T E H C I N N A A
H I A N A M K T R E E E
O S L L F N H U E P S H
A E E W L A N S B G Y H
T N H R U E S A A O T C
O E A O H O M M H C S R
H C W O L T W A C O G A
T A T G H E C A T L J T
A C H A P I D T I E O U
R R O L V I W M M E E L
A A R T S I M H Y T I P
S N N S R E A E A E N Y
E E E E R D O N H E N T
A R S U I V A L F B A O
C S S I N T A K W N M E
```

4. OLD TESTAMENT

Find all the biblical books hiding in the grid. The leftover letters spell a quote by Theodore Roosevelt.

AMOS
CHRONICLES
DANIEL
DEUTERONOMY
ECCLESIASTES
ESTHER
EXODUS
EZEKIEL
EZRA
GENESIS
HABAKKUK
HAGGAI
HOSEA
ISAIAH
JEREMIAH
JOB
JOEL
JONAH

JOSHUA
JUDGES
KINGS
LAMENTATIONS
LEVITICUS
MALACHI
MICAH
NAHUM
NEHEMIAH
NUMBERS
OBADIAH
PROVERBS
PSALMS
SAMUEL
SONG OF SOLOMON
ZECHARIAH
ZEPHANIAH

```
S  E  T  S  A  I  S  E  L  C  C  E
A  A  T  L  G  E  N  E  S  I  S  H
M  O  R  E  E  J  O  S  H  U  A  L
U  O  L  V  S  E  I  E  U  S  E  E
E  G  E  I  T  Z  T  L  B  O  J  I
L  H  I  T  H  R  A  C  J  N  K  N
N  O  K  I  E  A  T  I  W  G  L  A
K  E  E  C  R  N  N  N  D  O  S  D
U  G  Z  U  E  A  E  O  O  F  O  Y
K  A  E  S  O  H  M  R  J  S  M  F
K  H  H  T  E  U  A  H  H  O  A  P
A  I  A  M  E  M  L  C  N  L  R  B
B  S  I  I  I  S  B  O  I  O  L  E
A  A  R  I  M  S  R  A  V  M  W  Z
H  I  A  O  R  E  G  E  A  O  T  E
H  A  H  M  T  G  R  L  B  N  O  P
R  H  C  U  A  B  A  E  S  M  S  H
E  T  E  H  S  C  H  M  J  U  U  A
A  D  Z  N  H  A  L  C  D  O  L  N
L  H  A  I  D  A  B  O  E  G  E  I
K  I  N  G  S  E  X  D  U  C  A  A
T  I  O  P  S  E  G  D  U  J  N  H
```

5. ASTRONAUTS A-C

Find all the astronauts hiding in the grid.
The leftover letters spell a quote by Neil Armstrong.

ADAMSON	BUCHLI
AKERS	BULL
ALDRIN	BURSCH
ALLEN	CALDEIRO
ALTMAN	CAREY
ARMSTRONG	CARR
ASHBY	CERNAN
BAGIAN	CHAPMAN
BAKER	CHAWLA
BARRY	CHIAO
BEAN	CLARK
BLAHA	CLEAVE
BLOOMFIELD	CLIFFORD
BLUFORD	COATS
BOBKO	COLLINS
BORMAN	CONRAD
BOWERSOX	COOPER
BRADY	COVEY
BRAND	CRIPPEN
BRIDGES	CULBERTSON
BROWN	CURBEAM

```
M Y S Y E V O C B T N E
A R L Y C K L U L R A E
L B L A B I C L O A M T
W A U O F H B B O E R S
A K B F L W L E M O O K
H E O I Y N A R F D B E
C R W R D D H T I A N C
D U E D A C A S E W A Y
O B R M R A S O L L R E
N R S B B R A N D R M R
C O O P E R B E A N S A
N W X K D A I B L B T C
A N A E G R M B L S R R
M R I I O S U U E T O I
P H A E C R F G N B N P
A N A S S O D A I S G P
H S O C R I N F M A E E
C N H D R R A R S V D N
H O E B E S M I A R E T
I O A C Y U T E N D D E
A R S T C O L L I N S T
O A N D S C A L D R I N
```

6. LIVE MÁS

Find all the foods hiding in the grid. The leftover letters spell a quote by Lupita Nyong'o.

ARROZ CON POLLO

BURRITO

CARNE ASADA

CARNITAS

CEVICHE

CHILE RELLENO

CHORIZO

CHURRO

DULCE DE LECHE

EMPANADA

ENCHILADA

FLAN

FLAUTA

FRIJOLES

GORDITA

HUEVOS
  RANCHEROS

JÍCAMA

MENUDO

MOLE

NACHOS

PICO DE GALLO

POZOLE

QUESADILLA

QUESO

SOPE

TACO

TAMALE

TAQUITOS

TORTA

TORTILLAS

TOSTADA

```
E  V  A  M  A  C  I  J  E  S  R  Y
Q  S  O  E  N  C  H  I  L  A  D  A
U  L  Q  U  E  S  A  D  I  L  L  A
E  H  C  E  L  E  D  E  C  L  U  D
S  O  H  C  A  N  I  N  H  I  S  A
O  T  I  R  R  U  B  T  I  T  A  N
R  Z  A  G  L  E  A  A  L  R  T  A
E  L  I  C  A  S  R  M  E  O  I  P
H  T  U  R  O  N  R  A  R  T  N  M
C  O  D  P  O  Z  O  L  E  A  R  E
N  S  E  R  O  H  Z  E  L  M  A  A
A  T  U  A  L  F  C  F  L  T  C  C
R  A  G  R  O  H  O  C  E  E  R  A
S  D  T  Y  U  S  N  T  N  O  R  R
O  A  E  R  E  G  P  S  O  V  E  N
V  D  R  R  O  Y  O  T  H  E  I  E
E  O  U  N  G  T  L  R  I  H  S  A
U  C  A  N  I  L  L  L  D  C  E  S
H  D  L  U  E  U  O  P  I  I  T  A
A  I  Q  N  M  M  E  X  I  V  T  D
C  A  O  F  R  I  J  O  L  E  S  A
T  O  L  L  A  G  E  D  O  C  I  P
```

7. GEMSTONES

Find all the gemstones hiding in the grid. The leftover letters spell a quote by Elizabeth Taylor.

AGATE

ALEXANDRITE

AMBER

AMETHYST

AQUAMARINE

AZURITE

BERYL

BLOODSTONE

CITRINE

DIAMOND

EMERALD

GARNET

HEMATITE

HESSONITE

JADE

KUNZITE

LAPIS LAZULI

MOONSTONE

OPAL

PEARL

QUARTZ

RHODOLITE

RUBY

SAPPHIRE

SARDONYX

TANZANITE

TOPAZ

TOURMALINE

TURQUOISE

ZIRCON

```
I  T  A  D  D  O  A  E  R  E  W  E
L  A  P  O  I  A  G  Z  D  R  L  S
E  N  I  R  A  M  A  U  Q  A  B  A
N  Z  I  N  M  P  T  G  P  L  J  P
O  A  G  E  O  M  E  I  O  E  S  P
T  N  B  T  N  U  S  O  Z  X  T  H
S  I  C  N  D  L  D  T  Y  A  O  I
N  T  T  I  A  S  R  B  B  N  E  R
O  E  K  Z  T  A  U  C  E  D  A  E
O  U  U  O  U  R  S  E  E  R  T  N
M  L  N  Q  R  D  I  T  A  I  Y  I
I  E  Z  H  Q  O  I  N  M  T  E  L
Y  A  I  R  U  N  E  M  E  E  I  A
N  E  T  Y  O  Y  O  U  T  T  C  M
A  N  E  S  I  X  E  I  H  I  T  R
P  O  S  P  S  M  R  S  Y  L  S  U
E  E  S  S  E  U  R  N  S  O  A  O
H  D  I  R  Z  A  O  A  T  D  N  T
C  E  A  A  E  C  R  Y  O  O  U  C
A  L  N  O  R  B  N  L  L  H  Y  A
D  E  T  I  T  A  M  E  H  R  D  M
I  R  Z  T  E  N  R  A  G  E  I  T
```

8. GREEK GODS

Find all the mythological names hiding in the grid.
The leftover letters spell a quote and its speaker.

AETHER

APHRODITE

APOLLO

ARES

ARTEMIS

ATHENA

CHRONOS

DEMETER

DIONYSUS

EREBUS

EROS

GAEA

HADES

HEMERA

HEPHAESTUS

HERA

HERMES

HESTIA

HYPNOS

METIS

NYX

PONTUS

POSEIDON

TARTARUS

THANATOS

TYCHE

URANUS

ZEUS

```
H E M E R A T H E N A
E Z T A R T A R U S T
R E H I E B X A T T L
M U E F D Y E I E S L
E S U T N O P R I U D
S O N P Y H R M O T I
S U S A S C E H C S E
N U S E S T H O P E F
C O N Y R O S E R A N
S T A A N N N E T H C
H A O S R O B O T P H
E W N I N U I G R E T
N E O R S S E D A H W
I L D L I B E T A E C
H E I T O N E N W R A
H O E A C O A N T A R
O M S I L T S T E P H
A T O T O C H T A O O
S N P S A P H O L L E
R E T E M E D O N L B
O N A H R P A R T O E
```

9. ROMAN GODS

Find all the mythological names hiding in the grid.
The leftover letters spell a quote and its speaker.

AGDISTIS	LUNA
APOLLO	MARS
AURORA	MERCURY
BELLONA	MINERVA
CERES	NEPTUNE
CONSUS	ORCUS
CUPID	PALES
DIANA	POMONA
FERONIA	PROSERPINA
FLORA	QUIRINUS
FORTUNA	SATURN
JANUS	TELLUS
JUNO	TERMINUS
JUPITER	VESTA
LARES	VORTUMNUS
LIBER	VULCAN
LUCINA	

```
W  H  E  N  F  E  R  O  N  I  A  A
R  C  H  L  A  C  E  O  L  O  G  I
S  T  O  S  O  D  R  L  I  S  C  O
M  R  V  N  E  R  A  E  T  H  T  E
A  V  S  M  I  R  S  S  B  I  E  N
R  U  E  G  E  A  R  M  S  I  L  O
S  I  T  S  I  D  G  A  N  U  L  F
U  U  V  E  T  E  R  M  I  N  U  S
N  O  N  U  J  A  E  N  C  U  S  S
M  D  B  I  P  E  T  S  E  L  A  P
U  M  E  O  R  P  I  I  R  L  O  T
T  H  L  E  O  I  P  Y  E  W  E  I
R  L  L  M  S  L  U  S  S  N  L  F
O  A  O  I  E  N  J  Q  U  D  S  H
V  N  N  E  R  W  A  T  C  N  S  W
A  U  A  A  P  E  P  A  R  L  A  R
U  T  L  I  I  E  N  G  O  U  V  J
R  R  B  C  N  D  I  P  U  C  R  O
O  O  X  S  A  T  U  R  N  I  E  I
R  F  N  G  G  N  L  O  V  N  N  E
A  S  J  O  H  N  B  A  R  A  I  R
Y  M  O  R  Y  R  U  C  R  E  M  E
```

10. WINNING SPELLING WORDS

Find all the words hiding in the grid. The leftover letters spell a quote and its speaker.

ASCETICISM

CAMBIST

CHLOROPHYLL

DÉMARCHE

DULCIMER

ECZEMA

ELEGIACAL

EUDAEMONIC

EUONYM

FIBRANNE

FOULARD

FRACAS

GUERDON

INCISOR

KNACK

KNAIDEL

LUGE

LUXURIANCE

LYCEUM

MACULATURE

MILIEU

PURIM

RATOON

SCHAPPE

SERREFINE

SHALLOON

SMARAGDINE

STROMUHR

TORSION

VIGNETTE

XANTHOSIS

```
C O L U X U R I A N C E
A M P E H C R A M E D N
S C H A P P E A R N Y I
C A M B I S T U N A M F
E H E I S W T I T H S E
T O L F R A C A S L I R
I U T O L U C L E A S R
C A R U R P P R R C O E
I O C N N O O L L A H S
S A U N R S P C I I T C
M M I L I E U H R G N I
U A A C T M M H Y E A N
E I N R Y O U I N L X O
C I N N A M E Z C E L M
Y O O E O G R N S L P E
L U O R N K D O E L U A
E E T T E N G I V L I D
D S A N G A A S N G W U
I O R N U C T R L E A E
A S T D L K A O B V I D
N O D R E U G T R I U S
K E N K D R A L U O F O
```

11. SCI-FI NOVELS

Find all the books hiding in the grid. The leftover letters spell a quote and its source.

AMPED

BATTLEFIELD EARTH

BRAVE NEW WORLD

CHILDREN [OF THE MIND]

CONGO

CONTACT

DEMON

DUNE

ENDER'S GAME

GATEWAY

GULF

IDLEWILD

JURASSIC PARK

LIGHT

MATTER

NEEDLE

NOVA

OMEGA

POLARIS

[THE] POSITRONIC [MAN]

PREY

RENDEZVOUS [WITH RAMA]

SIGNAL

SPHERE

SPIN

[A PLANET CALLED] TREASON

UBIK

VALIS

VENUS

VURT

[THE] WAR OF THE WORLDS

WASP

[A] WRINKLE IN TIME

XENOCIDE

```
J U R A S S I C P A R K
A R E N D E Z V O U S X
R E E Y O L U T E N L E
L I M T A P N G D M G N
E Y A N T S R L O B U O
P B G E U A I E I A L C
O I S R T W M R Y T A I
S T R D E A I M A T E D
I M E L M R T D G L D E
T A D I I O C L E E O S
R I N H T F A R M F C P
O H E C N T T O O I N H
N I N O I H N W A E O E
I E V O E E O W M L S R
C A U T L W C E P D A E
O F A D K O D N E E E E
L O E R N R E E D A R A
N E B S I L A V U R T A
N C K P R D T A N T H O
T H E I W S F R E H G U
T V E N U S U B I K I U
R E Y A W E T A G U L F
```

12. PLANT GENERA

Find all the genera hiding in the grid. The leftover letters spell a quote and its speaker.

ACACIA
ALLIUM
ANTHURIUM
ARDISIA
ASTRAGALUS
CAREX
CASSIA
CENTAUREA
CROTON
CYPERUS
DENDROBIUM
ERIA
ERICA
EUCALYPTUS
EUGENIA
EUPHORBIA

FICUS
HABENARIA
INDIGOFERA
IPOMOEA
IXORA
MICONIA
OXALIS
PEPEROMIA
PIPER
QUERCUS
SALVIA
SENECIO
SILENE
SOLANUM
SYZYGIUM

```
S  J  S  E  I  X  O  R  A  U  A  S
O  T  M  U  I  L  L  A  E  R  I  A
L  L  H  C  L  I  V  R  I  P  S  N
A  I  C  A  C  A  I  N  O  C  I  M
N  G  I  L  B  C  G  M  S  N  D  P
U  N  N  Y  A  E  O  A  D  O  R  T
M  E  O  P  N  E  N  I  R  O  A  U
U  G  C  T  A  H  G  A  O  T  I  N
I  E  Y  U  O  O  M  U  R  S  S  T
G  H  P  S  F  R  X  A  V  I  S  A
Y  E  E  E  A  A  C  A  S  U  A  I
Z  M  R  N  S  L  I  A  L  H  C  M
Y  A  U  I  N  E  V  N  R  I  F  O
S  N  S  I  R  E  E  I  E  E  S  R
U  T  D  O  B  M  A  N  A  G  X  E
C  H  D  A  L  O  I  T  T  L  U  P
R  U  E  A  I  B  R  O  H  P  U  E
E  R  F  L  S  O  W  D  E  R  N  P
U  I  A  E  R  U  A  T  N  E  C  H
Q  U  A  N  S  C  C  H  L  E  R  I
S  M  T  I  A  N  A  I  N  D  D  E
O  I  C  E  N  E  S  R  F  S  E  N
```

Answer on page 172.

13. POPES, PART I

Find all the papal names hiding in the grid.
The leftover letters spell a quote and its speaker.

ANACLETUS

ANASTASIUS

ANICETUS

BONIFACE

CAIUS

CALLIXTUS

CELESTINE

CLEMENT

CORNELIUS

DAMASUS

DIONYSIUS

ELEUTERUS

EUSEBIUS

FABIAN

FELIX

HYGINUS

JULIUS

LEO

LIBERIUS

LINUS

LUCIUS

MARK

MILTIADES

PONTIAN

PETER

PIUS

SIXTUS

SOTER

STEPHEN

SYLVESTER

URBAN

VICTOR

ZEPHYRINUS

```
T R E T S E V L Y S H E
F O A C T S T H U A T I
W T A S S U N I G Y H N
A C G L I T R R L N A E
S I V U P E T E R B E R
U V D C B L Z S R D A M
I A G I B C E U E D M Y
L A L U O A P T M B I T
E I O S N N H X I L E F
N N S T I A Y I O B R M
R E A D F C R S P O E I
O P E A A E I K I A T L
C O R M C L N R N U O T
A A S A E E U A F N S I
L E U S M S S M A P U A
L E T U U T R U B O R D
I O E S A I S R I E E E
X W C S I N B U A L T S
T L I L A E C E N P U A
U U N E H P E T S I E J
S N A I T N O P A U L T
H T N E M E L C E S E R
```

14. POPES, PART II

Find all the papal names hiding in the grid.
The leftover letters spell a tweet from Pope Francis.

ADEODATUS
ADRIAN
AGAPETUS
AGATHO
BENEDICT
CONON
CONSTANTINE
DONUS
EUGENE
FORMOSUS
HORMISDAS
JOHN
MARINUS
MARTIN
NICHOLAS

PASCHAL
PAUL
PELAGIUS
ROMANUS
SABINIAN
SERGIUS
SEVERINUS
SILVERIUS
SISINNIUS
THEODORE
VALENTINE
VIGILIUS
VITALIAN
ZACHARY

```
I  T  I  S  S  U  I  L  I  G  I  V
C  D  B  Y  G  O  D  S  M  E  I  N
P  O  E  R  O  D  O  E  H  T  H  I
E  N  N  O  H  T  A  G  A  O  R  C
L  U  C  S  C  Y  T  L  J  H  A  H
A  S  O  T  T  S  I  W  E  A  R  O
G  E  N  S  Z  A  C  H  A  R  Y  L
I  A  O  E  N  D  N  A  I  R  D  A
U  V  N  N  E  S  D  T  M  A  Y  S
S  A  B  I  N  I  A  N  I  W  E  N
I  E  V  T  T  M  E  F  R  N  T  S
S  I  S  N  C  R  A  O  R  E  E  U
I  S  I  E  I  O  A  R  O  S  F  I
N  U  L  L  D  H  D  M  I  U  S  G
N  N  V  A  E  P  E  O  R  N  E  R
I  I  E  V  N  N  O  S  L  A  U  E
U  R  R  A  E  D  D  U  A  M  I  S
S  E  I  G  B  N  A  S  H  O  G  T
H  V  U  I  S  L  T  J  C  R  O  Y
F  E  S  U  L  M  U  E  S  S  S  A
G  S  E  T  O  T  S  A  A  H  E  W
O  R  L  D  S  U  T  E  P  A  G  A
```

15. ASTRONAUTS D-I

Find all the astronauts hiding in the grid. The leftover letters spell a quote by John Glenn.

DAVIS
DUFFY
DUKE
DUNBAR
DUTTON
EDWARDS
EISELE
ENGLE
EVANS
FABIAN
FOALE
FREEMAN
FULLERTON
GARAN
GARDNER
GARRIOTT
GEMAR
GIBSON
GIVENS
GLENN

GODWIN
GORDON
GORIE
GRABE
GRAVELINE
GRIGGS
HAISE
HARRIS
HART
HAUCK
HAWLEY
HELMS
HENIZE
HENRICKS
HERRINGTON
HIEB
HILMERS
HOBAUGH
HOFFMAN
IVINS

```
H B I N D F D A V I S O
E E H O B A U G H N N T
N I R T E B K I A K A N
R H S R N I E B R F V O
I W W E I A S S R R E H
C K A L L N G O I E T Y
K O C L E E G N S E U C
S O U U V R I T L M D S
D N A F A Y R F O A L E
R A I B R H G B O N S U
A T N V G O R D O N R A
W U E S I A H D E A E A
D U F F Y Y R V I M M N
E N G L E W I A H F L I
C N E A T G H Y N F I O
U E M H R H A R E O H V
E L A S A R E Z E H E N
E G R W H N I N F B O O
U R L E D N R O A T B E
A E L R E U O R T T I F
Y M A H U L G U S T U N
S G S E G O D W I N T S
```

16. "FAMILY GUY"

Find all the "Family Guy" names hiding in the grid.
The leftover letters spell a quote and its speaker.

BONNIE

BRIAN

CHRIS

CLEVELAND

CONSUELA

DIANE SIMMONS

DR. ELMER
    HARTMAN

ERNIE [THE GIANT
    CHICKEN]

[THE] EVIL MONKEY

JOE

JOHN HERBERT

JOYCE KINNEY

LOIS

LORETTA

MAYOR ADAM WEST

MEG

MORT

MURIEL

NEIL

PETER

[CARTER]
    PEWTERSCHMIDT

QUAGMIRE

RUPERT

SEAMUS LEVINE

STEWIE

TOM TUCKER

TRICIA TAKANAWA

```
S E A M U S L E V I N E
T H E O N O L Y R T O C
K P I K R N O W T S H A
T E S E T A Y S S E T E
D W T A D Y T H E W O N
I T C R E K C U T M O T
A E A O E R I M G A U Q
N R W L N Y I E N D S T
E S A I T S M D U A T I
S C N O J N U R I R K N
I H A L O I S E O O D W
M M K Y Y S L L L Y N T
M I A E C I T M H A A A
O D T K E R B E T M L W
N T A N K H O R W O E R
S R I O I C N H K I V S
I E C M N S N A N T E H
E P I L N A I R B F L A
M U R I E L E T M I C L
O R T V Y Y L M E E E I
R E T E P A C A O O C C
T R E B R E H N H O J A
```

17. ITALIAN FOOD

Find all the Italian food hiding in the grid.
The leftover letters spell a quote and its speaker.

BUCATINI	OSSOBUCO
CAPELLINI	PANCETTA
CAPICOLA	PAPPARDELLE
CARBONARA	PECORINO
CAVATAPPI	PENNE
CIABATTA	PIZZA
FARFALLE	PROSCIUTTO
FETTUCCINE	RAVIOLI
FUSILLI	RICOTTA
GNOCCHI	RIGATONI
LASAGNE	RISOTTO
MACARONI	SALAMI
MARINARA	SPAGHETTI
ORECCHIETTE	TAGLIATELLE
ORZO	ZITI

```
N O I M A L A S M A T T
E E E R A T T A B A I C
T W H L E C L R O E I V
T E B E L O A E Z N O V
E E R R C A S R R E E A
I L L I S U F S O L O C
H T P C H E E R L N N A
C A F O O Z T E A O I P
C D S T I T T I L F R E
E N M T K A U S A O O L
R L I A I E C X S A C L
O I L L R C C C A T E I
E S G E P I I T G T P N
I A S A D U N I N E N I
T R G O T R E A E C I T
T A N T B O A T R N E A
E N O T A U N P P A N C
H O C O L Y C I P P N U
G B C S C A Z O R A E B
A R H I M Z E N E L P E
P A I R A V I O L I C T
S C A V A T A P P I R A
```

18. FINDING MY RELIGION

Find all the religions hiding in the grid. The leftover letters spell a quote and its speaker.

ADVENTIST

ANGLICAN

BAHA'I

BAPTIST

BUDDHISM

CANDOMBLÉ

CHRISTIANITY

CHURCH OF CHRIST, [SCIENTIST]

EPISCOPAL

FAISM

HINDUISM

ISLAM

JAINISM

LUTHERAN

MANDAEISM

NON-DENOMINATIONAL

NUOISM

PAGANISM

PRESBYTERIANISM

RASTAFARIANISM

SANTERIA

SHINTO

SIKHISM

SPIRITUALISM

TAOISM

WICCA

WUISM

```
Y T I N A I T S I R H C
Y T S I T N E V D A O H
U C A B U D D H I S M U
N A R E H T U L H T N R
O N O T B E L I I A E C
N A C I L G N A M F V H
D E N I W T N G S A M O
E O D U O A U M I R S F
N L I N O O S T E I I C
O S B I W I C C A A N H
M L E M H S S Y D N A R
I S P K O M O M N I I I
N M I U B D S E A S R S
A S S L L I N I M M E T
T E C I A V E A I S T S
I N O F N U Y O C I Y I
O B P U R I T S E U B T
N L A F S W A I A D S P
A M L H I V I J R N E A
L V E K A M A L S I R B
P A G A N I S M A H P N
A N D A A I R E T N A S
```

19. KITCHEN AIDS

Find all the kitchen equipment hiding in the grid.
The leftover letters spell an anonymous prayer.

APPLE CORER

BASTER

BISCUIT CUTTER

CAN OPENER

COLANDER

CORKSCREW

EGG SEPARATOR

EGG SLICER

FOOD MILL

FUNNEL

GARLIC PRESS

LADLE

MEAT
THERMOMETER

MORTAR AND
PESTLE

NUTCRACKER

OVEN MITTS

PASTRY BLENDER

PEELER

PEPPER MILL

PIE WEIGHTS

REAMER

RICER

ROLLING PIN

SIFTER

SPATULA

SPIDER

TONGS

WHISK

ZESTER

```
R E L E E P B M L E S S
E R R R R T R E A M E R
K S E E P R H A E M F E
C P C T A O E T O O D R
A I I T S I F T E R O O
R D L U T E B H S T E C
C E S C R F Z E A A O E
T R G T Y R G R E R B L
U U G I B S A M C A T P
N H E U L P R O A N E P
F N A C E K L M N D E A
M I P S N S I E O P I L
Y P G I D I C T P E B E
W G S B E H P E E S O I
E N L D R W R R N T V A
R I E L U M E S E L E L
C L A N I D S I R E N U
S L D L N M S T G H M T
K O L A E L D O V H I A
R R L E B E T O W E T P
O O E N U S G N O T T S
C L A D L E N N U F S S
```

20. LAKES

Find all the "lakes" hiding in the grid.
The leftover letters spell a quote by Garrison Keillor.
Even though all the answers have "Lake"
in their full names, four are reservoirs,
one is an estuary, and one is subglacial.

ALBERT
ATHABASCA
BAIKAL
CHAMPLAIN
COMO
DEVIL'S
ERIE
GARDA
GREAT BEAR
HURON
KENTUCKY
LADOGA
MALAWI
MEAD
MICHIGAN

NIPIGON
ONEGA
ONTARIO
PONTCHARTRAIN
POWELL
RAINY
SAKAKAWEA
TABLE ROCK
TAHOE
TAYMYR
TITICACA
VICTORIA
VOSTOK
WINNIPEG

```
A G O D A L W E R L C O
M I E T O O L A Y K E W
T O R B E V N Y M G M O
N R W O O H K T Y L I E
R E E S T C A L A L C T
S R T B U C H K T R H E
A O A T L W I O M E I N
K O N E G A I V N A G O
A E R E B S T W I R A O
K N G A L T L R A I N Y
A C T H E M A E R L N A
W H R E G O O E T D A L
E A S L I V E D R O O M
A M K I N T G A A G C A
C P N D A A L C H E O L
S L T H E B C A C P M H
A A L I L L D C T I O R
B I G E E E N I N N A R
A N A E W R A T O N E B
H U R O N O G I P I N O
T V D E A C P T R W V E
A R A A G K E E O H A T
```

21. DOG BREED PLACES

Find all the dog breed words hiding in the grid.
The leftover letters spell a quote and its speaker.

ALASKAN
AMERICAN
AUSTRALIAN
BOSTON
BRITTANY
BRUSSELS
CHIHUAHUA
ENGLISH
FRENCH
GERMAN
IRISH
JAPANESE

LABRADOR
MANCHESTER
NEWFOUNDLAND
NORWEGIAN
PORTUGUESE
PYRENEES
SCOTTISH
SIBERIAN
SWEDISH
TIBETAN
WELSH
YORKSHIRE

```
N E W F O U N D L A N D
A O I A M C A O U L L L
M E R D A D O S T A H G
R A B W E C T A U S P S
E E N I E R F A I K O W
G S N C A G O R N A R B
T H E L H O I S E N T R
W H I N O E H A G H U U
E A I R A S S V N C G S
N E A O I P N T M N U S
G E M D A N A Y E E E E
L T E A H I I J N R S L
I W R R G I R Y E F E S
S I B P A E T B R E C
H T C A H O B R I E H O
S E A L W H I H N I O T
R E N F U T S E H S E T
A N D I T K R U S E T I
M Y T A R Y A E E T H S
I N N O P H R W E L S H
A Y Y S U C A L S D I O
G E N A T E B I T N E S
```

22. MOVIE MUSICALS

Find all the musicals hiding in the grid. The leftover letters spell a lyric from "Nature Boy," which was featured in the movie "Moulin Rouge."

AN AMERICAN IN PARIS

ANNIE

A STAR IS BORN

BRIGADOON

CABARET

CHICAGO

DAMN YANKEES

DREAMGIRLS

EVITA

FAME

FUNNY GIRL

GIGI

GREASE

GYPSY

HAIR

MARY POPPINS

MEET ME IN ST. LOUIS

MY FAIR LADY

OKLAHOMA!

OLIVER!

ON THE TOWN

SHOW BOAT

SWEET CHARITY

THE KING AND I

THE SOUND OF MUSIC

TOMMY

VICTOR/VICTORIA

```
T S L R I G M A E R D H
E G R E A O G I T E S C
T T H I L D T R N G Y A
O C H I C A G O E U L B
S L V M C M M T M A E A
I E V E I N Y C E M S R
R R L E S Y F I A E Y E
A A R T U A A V M N S T
P I S M M N I R O J W H
N F U E F K R O H S E E
I M U I O E L T A T E K
N A N N D E A C L T T I
A R W S N S D I K A C N
C Y O T U Y Y V O E H G
I P T L O O G B V L A A
R O E O S O W I V E R N
E P H U E O T A R N I D
M P T I H A I R D L T I
A I N S T B E I L O Y V
N N O O D A G I R B E D
A S T A R I S B O R N I
N R E T G Y P S Y U R N
```

23. DOWN ON THE PHARM

Find all the drugs hiding in the grid. The leftover letters spell a quote and its speaker.

ABILIFY

ACTOS

ADVAIR

ALIMTA

ATRIPLA

AVASTIN

AVONEX

CELEBREX

COPAXONE

CRESTOR

CYMBALTA

DIOVAN

ENBREL

EVISTA

GLEEVEC

HERCEPTIN

HUMIRA

IDAMYCIN

IMURAN

JANUVIA

LANTUS

LEVEMIR

LUCENTIS

NAMENDA

NASONEX

NEXIUM

NIASPAN

OXYCONTIN

REBIF

RITUXAN

SPIRIVA

STELARA

SYMBICORT

SYNAGIS

TAMIFLU

TRUVADA

VICTOZA

VYVANSE

XGEVA

XOLAIR

ZETIA

```
X E N O V A D A V U R T
E W L T A L V R X K A V
N I E N A A I I E G T Y
O I R A S M D M R A R V
S A B I E F I N B I I A
A B N V N S I F E I P N
N I E U O U O B L M L S
I L X N X T N T E U A E
A I I A A N I N C R R N
S F U J P A T E Y A I A
P Y M S O L N N M N M X
A B M E C T O I B I U U
N S T B I V C T A T H T
A N M S I I Y P L S E I
V I D T S C X E T A I R
O C G E Y T O C A V C O
I Y L L N O L R I A A T
D M E A A Z A E T V L S
I A E R G A I H E N I E
A D V A I R R G Z E M R
H I E I S P X P O C T C
R A C T E E V I S T A S
```

24. CHESS OPENINGS

Find all the chess-related answers hiding in the grid. The leftover letters spell a quote and its speaker.

ALEKHINE

BENKO GAMBIT

BENONI

BUDAPEST

CARO-KANN

CATALAN

DUTCH

ENGLISH

FRENCH

GIUOCO PIANO

GRÜNFELD

KING'S GAMBIT

KING'S INDIAN

LARSEN

NIMZO-INDIAN

PETROFF

PHILIDOR

PIRC

QUEEN'S GAMBIT

QUEEN'S INDIAN

RÉTI

RUY LOPEZ

SCOTCH

SICILIAN

SLAV

VIENNA

```
O  I  B  U  D  A  P  E  S  T  G  T
E  N  G  L  I  S  H  E  T  I  I  M
R  L  A  R  S  E  N  O  R  B  E  U
P  E  S  I  E  T  V  I  M  M  A  C
T  D  T  L  P  O  N  A  S  A  I  A
N  U  G  I  A  O  G  T  L  G  O  T
T  T  R  H  N  O  C  E  R  S  T  A
H  C  I  E  K  N  H  O  G  G  S  L
T  H  B  N  H  C  K  A  U  N  N  A
Q  U  E  E  N  S  I  N  D  I  A  N
U  B  C  E  I  H  N  E  S  K  G  S
E  I  R  A  M  L  G  W  A  Y  R  S
E  F  P  G  Z  E  S  T  U  P  U  S
N  E  E  H  O  T  I  W  H  E  N  N
S  A  T  V  I  E  N  N  A  N  F  I
G  L  R  L  N  L  D  O  H  N  E  S
A  E  O  E  D  A  I  T  C  A  L  M
M  K  F  O  I  N  A  D  T  K  D  O
B  H  F  P  A  O  N  L  O  O  Y  M
I  I  A  G  N  N  U  S  C  R  C  A
T  N  A  I  L  I  C  I  S  A  R  L
Z  E  P  O  L  Y  U  R  S  C  E  N
```

25. ASTRONAUTS J-O

Find all the astronauts hiding in the grid.
The leftover letters spell a quote and its speaker.

JEMISON	MCBRIDE
JERNIGAN	MCCOOL
JETT	MCCULLEY
JOHNSON	MCNAIR
JONES	MEADE
KELLY	MELNICK
KERWIN	MELROY
KILRAIN	MICHEL
KREGEL	MITCHELL
LAWRENCE	MORGAN
LENOIR	MUSGRAVE
LIND	NAGEL
LINENGER	NELSON
LLEWELLYN	NEWMAN
LOCKHART	NOWAK
LORIA	O'CONNOR
LOUNGE	OEFELEIN
LOVELL	O'LEARY
LUCID	ONIZUKA
MAGNUS	OSWALD
MATTINGLY	OVERMYER

```
E D A E M N A G R O M L
A N N M A T T I N G L Y
J O N I Z U K A R N G U
O S W A L D A R N O G E
H I N Y L L E W E L L I
N M S K E L L Y W G A V
S E C N O V E R M Y E R
O J O N O W A K A C D L
N I I A A O C R N D I O
R U S G L I F E I N R V
R N O E N M R C E E B E
O M A L U W U N L L C L
T R E G A L G E E S M L
Y M R L I E S P F O L A
M C C O R N L S E N O J
E A L C N O R W O I C E
M I G O U I Y E L A K T
I L I N O L W A J R H T
C M G N U C L R S L A B
H E U O R S C E E I R R
E V A R G S U M Y K T O
L L E H C T I M U G H S
```

Answer on page 176.

26. SPICE IT UP

Find all the Spice Islands products hiding in the grid. The leftover letters spell a quote by General Norman Schwarzkopf.

ANISE SEED

[SWEET] BASIL

BAY LEAVES

[WHOLE] CARAWAY SEED

[WHOLE] CELERY SEED

CHILI POWDER

[SNIPPED] CHIVES

CILANTRO

CINNAMON [STICKS]

[GROUND] CLOVES

[GROUND] CUMIN [SEED]

[SPICY] CURRY POWDER

DILL [WEED]

FENNEL SEED

[GROUND] GINGER

LEMON [PEEL]

MARJORAM

MUSTARD SEED

[GROUND] NUTMEG

OREGANO

PAPRIKA

PARSLEY

POPPY SEED

ROSEMARY

SAGE

SESAME SEED

TARRAGON

THYME

TURMERIC

```
A N D E E S E S I N A S
Y M A R J O R A M K A E
S U C L O V E S I G O S
L S U I D I E R E R W A
B T R O L R P M T L H M
C A R A W A Y S E E D E
H R Y H P H N M I I E S
I D P L T G O T L S E E
L S O C E N E L R S S E
I E W H A A I M L O L D
P E D I T S V M T H E O
O D E V U L D E U U N B
W E R E G N I G S C N E
D E E S Y P P O P A E N
E S T I W A R T A C F N
R Y D S T I L A I L O T
H R O S E M A R Y E N R
E E A R E L E R T H A I
N L G S I M W A O R G T
Y E L S R A P G H F E I
G C A U H T I O N G R F
O B T R C I N N A M O N
```

27. PAINT COLORS

Find all the Benjamin Moore colors hiding in the grid. The leftover letters spell a quote by Edward Hopper.

BATH SALTS

[CORAL] BUFF

CANDY STRIPE

COMET

COOL AQUA

FREESIA

FROSTY LIME

GALAXY

HEATHER PLUM

JACK FROST

JAVA

KIWI

LEMON TWIST

LUXE

MISTY ROSE

MYSTICAL GRAPE

PEACH JAM

PEPPERMINT

PLATINUM [GRAY]

POMEGRANATE

PROPOSAL

RASPBERRY
   MOUSSE

ROSE SILK

SANDBLAST

SILVER MIST

SKYLARK SONG

SUGARPLUM

TANGERINE DREAM

```
E I B F R O S E S I L K
M Y L A S O P O R P E O
I U T M T C E O U L M D
L S S U J H S A Y I O T
Y X A L A G S T I N N P
T W L P C N U A O R T E
S E B R K O O N L D W A
O P D A F S M G S T I C
R A N G R K Y E E S S H
F R A U O R R R T I T J
T G S S S A R I A L A A
H L F E T L E N N V T M
R A R E U Y B E A E N U
W C E X O K P D R R I L
U I E A I S S R G M M P
L T S W U D A E E I R R
B S I E N Q R A M S E E
O Y A B R E A M O T P H
A M U N I T A L P S P T
O F M I S T Y R O S E A
F N T O P A I N T O P E
E P I R T S Y D N A C H
```

28. POE STORIES

Find all the stories hiding in the grid. The leftover letters spell a paraphrasing of a quote by Edgar Allan Poe.

[THE] ASSIGNATION

BERENICE

[THE] BLACK CAT

BON-BON

[THE] BUSINESS MAN

[THE] DEVIL IN THE BELFRY

[THE] GOLD-BUG

HOP-FROG

KING PEST

[THE] LANDSCAPE GARDEN

LIGEIA

LIONIZING

LOSS OF BREATH

MORELLA

MYSTIFICATION

[THE] OBLONG BOX

[THE] PIT AND THE PENDULUM

[THE] POWER OF WORDS

[A] PREDICAMENT

[THE] SPECTACLES

[THE] SPHINX

```
N A M S S E N I S U B O
O F P X O B G N O L B O
I U N S I T S O M I H A
T S D B E E D I U O N S
A I E G I L R T L N A I
N K V L D T O A U I H A
G T I A T H W C D Z O S
I E L N W H F I N I O M
S O I D G S O F E N S T
S D N S U P R I P G I S
A L T C B H E T E S L P
I O H A D I W S H K R E
E S E P L N O Y T E C C
T S B E O X P M D I B T
H O E G G E M I N L A A
R F L A E O C E A N T C
H B F R O A R C T O S L
E R R D M E K F I B W E
H E Y E B C O A P N R S
E A N N A L L E R O M L
E T A T S T A B L B H E
T H O U T T E R T H E M
```

29. POKÉMON

Find all the Pokémon hiding in the grid.
The leftover letters spell a quote spoken by Jessie.

ABRA	MACHOP
ARBOK	MEOWTH
BEEDRILL	METAPOD
BULBASAUR	NINETALES
BUTTERFREE	ODDISH
CHARMANDER	ONIX
CHARMELEON	PARAS
CLEFABLE	PIDGEY
DITTO	PONYTA
DODRIO	RAICHU
EKANS	RATICATE
FEAROW	RATTATA
GLOOM	SANDSHREW
GOLBAT	SANDSLASH
GOLEM	SEEL
GRIMER	SLOWBRO
HYPNO	SNORLAX
IVYSAUR	SQUIRTLE
JIGGLYPUFF	WARTORTLE
JYNX	WEEDLE
KAKUNA	ZUBAT

```
W E R H S D N A S W D O
B U L B A S A U R O R J
U H C I A R E L P B L Y
T A B L O G C A W H A N
T A O E E G T O H Y N X
E L B A F E L C T P I A
R L L U M S S O W N N L
F E T I Z R N C O O E R
R F D R R E A T E M T O
E E U N O D K L M H A N
E L M P A T E O S E L S
T C D I Y M R E R E E Q
A P E E R L R A B P S U
C O A A E G G A W S H I
I H H R O W A G H P S R
T C I L A T N T I C A T
A A E O Y S T D C J L L
R M R N E A G I T I S E
B W O R A E F N D G D C
O P I V Y S A U R H N A
K A K U N A T A T T A R
O S O I R D O D D I S H
```

30. WHAT'S COOKING?

Find all the celebrity chefs hiding in the grid. The leftover letters spell a quote by Martha Stewart.

ANDERSON	KRIEGER
BATALI	LAGASSE
BAYLESS	LAWSON
BOURDAIN	MOOKING
BROWN	MORIMOTO
CHIARELLO	MOULTON
CHILD	NEELY
CORA	OLIVER
DEEN	PÉPIN
DE LAURENTIIS	RAY
DRUMMOND	ROCCA
FIERI	SÁNCHEZ
FLAY	STEWART
FLORENCE	SYMON
GARTEN	TSAI
GUARNASCHELLI	YEARWOOD
IRVINE	ZAKARIAN
KELLER	

```
I A B A T A L I G M K D
Z M I R E T R N O H R E
A C O U R V I R A G I E
K A N D I K I N I P E P
A S D N O M M U R D G E
R L E O O S F E R A E E
I L M T I I V A R N R C
A E O L I I I T T A T A
N K T U L T E A C E S S
O Y R O L N N C R B A O
S E A M E E O T O O N L
R A W S H R M T S U C L
E R E A C U Y R S R H E
D W T T S A S D E D E R
N O S W A L F F L A Z A
A O Y O N E E L Y I U I
R D O W R D S O A N H H
W I O N A E S R B Y B C
U R A Y U E A E S I N E
B E S S G N G N S A N D
M I A K T E A C I T S U
C F C R E L L E K E E D
```

Answer on page 177.

31. KNOTS

Find all the knot-related words hiding in the grid.
The leftover letters spell a quote and its speaker.

ANGLER'S

ARBOR

BACHMANN

BARREL

BEER

BOA

BUMPER

CORNED BEEF

DIAMOND

FALCONER'S

FIADOR

FISHERMAN'S

FRIENDSHIP

GRANNY

GRIEF

HONDA

JAMMING

LIGATURE

MATTHEW WALKER

MILLER'S

NAIL

PRATT

PRUSIK

SIMPLE

SLIP

SQUARE

STEIN

STEVEDORE

TARBUCK

THIEF

TRANSOM

TRIPLE CROWN

UNI

VERSATACKLE

WATER

```
W  W  R  E  P  M  U  B  H  E  N  Y
O  A  U  G  D  I  A  M  O  N  D  E
T  T  T  F  A  L  C  O  N  E  R  S
O  E  A  N  G  L  E  R  S  C  T  H
T  R  I  P  L  E  C  R  O  W  N  P
K  E  S  E  I  R  N  R  R  D  R  I
I  C  Q  N  O  S  N  F  Y  A  O  H
S  S  U  U  Y  E  R  R  T  O  B  S
U  T  A  B  D  N  P  T  E  O  T  D
R  E  R  B  R  I  N  E  A  A  K  N
P  V  E  R  S  A  T  A  C  K  L  E
N  E  K  R  L  O  T  T  R  R  A  I
F  D  L  N  U  I  D  H  O  G  A  R
I  O  A  N  G  T  A  D  O  N  N  F
S  R  W  F  B  D  A  N  R  N  A  E
H  E  W  E  N  I  N  G  A  N  L  P
E  A  E  O  F  T  N  M  I  P  I  K
R  R  H  L  I  I  H  E  M  L  N  D
M  B  T  E  M  C  T  I  S  L  A  N
A  O  T  M  A  S  S  O  E  R  O  O
N  R  A  B  S  G  R  I  E  F  E  V
S  J  M  O  S  N  A  R  T  E  L  T
```

Answer on page 177.

32. SUPER BOWL MVPS

Find all the athletes hiding in the grid. The leftover letters spell a quote and its speaker.

AIKMAN

ALLEN

ANDERSON

BILETNIKOFF

BRADSHAW

BRADY

BRANCH

BREES

BROWN

CSONKA

DAVIS

DAWSON

DENT

ELWAY

FLACCO

HARRIS

HOLMES

HOWLEY

JACKSON

LEWIS

MANNING

MARTIN

MONTANA

NAMATH

PLUNKETT

RICE

RIGGINS

RODGERS

RYPIEN

SCOTT

SIMMS

SMITH

STARR

STAUBACH

SWANN

WARD

WARNER

WILLIAMS

YOUNG

```
S R I B H C A B U A T S
B I L E T N I K O F F I
E C M L I B R O W N I V
D E R M M A R T I N E A
A K N O S C V E N A E D
W A H S D A R B E W T H
S N A E C G T A L S R B
O A N L A O E W L R D S
N T N W U P T R A E R B
E N S A A O W T S R L H
I O E Y M R S S S A D L
P M M D O A N F I T T I
Y M L A E U T E R W T S
R H O R N O N H R W E F
W I H B I N S G A S K L
T I I O R G I L H J N A
L B L E W A G N T A U C
T E R L I L N I G C L C
T H A K I N E C N K P O
A S M O C A C Y H S E R
G A A M E R M O N O W H
N I A N D E R S O N T E
```

33. HARRY POTTER

Find all the "Harry Potter" characters hiding in the grid. The leftover letters spell a quote spoken by Professor Dumbledore.

BARTY CROUCH
CEDRIC
CHO CHANG
CORNELIUS
DOLORES
DRACO MALFOY
DUDLEY
FENRIR
FLEUR
GILDEROY
GINNY
GODRIC
HAGRID
HARRY
HELGA
HERMIONE

KATIE BELL
LUNA
MAD-EYE MOODY
MCGONAGALL
NYMPHADORA
POMONA
REMUS
RITA
RON WEASLEY
ROWENA
SALAZAR
SEVERUS SNAPE
SIRIUS BLACK
SYBIL
VIKTOR
VOLDEMORT

```
I Y O F L A M O C A R D
R O W E N A C T I S O U
Y D O O M E Y E D A M R
C H M O I C E O D S H A
R O C R S Y L T H R R A
P T S O I O H O W I I M
H C U O R C Y T R A B C
W H A E I N T N W A H G
E T S R U U E F N T E O
A L E Y S F D L G I L N
R Y V A B R U E I R G A
O E E F L I D U L U A G
D I R G A H L R D A S A
A R U V C M E O E R A L
H E S I K H Y N R T L L
P H S K A S O N O O A C
M A N T U I U C Y R Z I
Y N A O M A B M H H A R
N U P R I L I T E A R D
L L E B E I T A K R N O
I H V O L D E M O R T G
R O N W E A S L E Y E S
```

Answer on page 178.

34. FRENCH FOOD

Find all the food items hiding in the grid.
The leftover letters spell a quote and its speaker.

AIOLI

BRIE

CAMEMBERT

CHÈVRE

COQ AU VIN

CRÈME BRÛLÉE

CRÊPE

ÉCLAIR

EMMENTAL

FOIE GRAS

FONDUE

GRATIN

GRUYÈRE

HARICOTS VERTS

MACARON

MOUSSE AU
  CHOCOLAT

POISSON

POMME DE TERRE

POT-AU-FEU

POULET

PROFITEROLE

QUICHE LORRAINE

RATATOUILLE

ROQUEFORT

SALADE NIÇOISE

SOUFFLÉ

TAPENADE

```
T E O U N S O U F F L E
D N T R O F E U Q O R E
R I S T A F U I N D E U
R A O P U O D R L P E Y
O R S A E I N I E O N U
H R T A S E O A D I I T
V O R E I G F L A S T A
P L E N O R T C N S A L
O E V I C A B E E O R O
E H S V I S A G P N G C
P C T U N E N N A E I O
R I O A E U O S T O R H
O U C Q D R E R V E H C
F Q I O A R F G R P E U
I L R C L N C R O H M A
T R A T A T O U I L L E
E M H T S A L Y D E I S
R L E I N E N E E R A S
O L B R T E I R B G H U
L T T R E B M E M A C O
E E L U R B E M E R C M
P O M M E D E T E R R E
```

35. ASTRONAUTS P-S

Find all the astronauts hiding in the grid.
The leftover letters spell a quote by Alan Shepard.

PAILES	SACCO
PARISE	SATCHER
PARKER	SCHIRRA
PATRICK	SCHMITT
PHILLIPS	SCOBEE
POGUE	SCOTT
POINDEXTER	SEARFOSS
POLANSKY	SEDDON
PRECOURT	SEGA
READDY	SHAW
REIGHTLER	SHEPARD
REILLY	SHRIVER
REISMAN	SMITH
RESNIK	SPRING
RICHARDS	STAFFORD
RIDE	STEWART
ROMINGER	STURCKOW
ROOSA	SULLIVAN
ROSS	SWIGERT

```
Y O T R A W E T S S U K
N D E O W B E I H P K N
N R S G Y D D A E R I A
A O I S T E R S P I N V
T F R P C R I A A N S I
L F A O I H T T R G E L
I A P H S R M E D I R L
N T C A I T I I A E S U
L S Y C R S M I T H W S
A Y K W M K S X R T T P
R H S A E H E I E T Y I
O E N H A D V R G O L L
M L A S N E T H I C L L
I W L I R I E S W S I I
N T O B O C C A S U E H
G P P K T R U O C E R P
E E B O C S F E U G O P
R I C H A R D S S I A N
O E S S A I U N S I T H
S E R E I G H T L E R W
S O S N O D D E S R G L
R E H C T A S O O R D A
```

Answer on page 178.

36. MOONS

Find all the moons hiding in the grid. The leftover letters spell a quote and its speaker.

ADRASTEA	HERSE
AITNE	IOCASTE
AMALTHEA	ISONOE
ANANKE	KALYKE
AOEDE	KORE
ARCHE	LEDA
AUTONOE	MEGACLITE
CALLIRRHOE	METIS
CALLISTO	MNEME
CARME	ORTHOSIE
CARPO	PASIPHAE
DEIMOS	PASITHEE
ELARA	PHOBOS
ERINOME	PRAXIDIKE
EUROPA	SINOPE
EURYDOME	SPONDE
GANYMEDE	TAYGETE
HARPALYKE	THEBE
HELIKE	THYONE
HERMIPPE	

```
C A L L I R R H O E A T
H M E T I S E E K U U R
E A D E A R T I S R T H
E L A I S R D S O Y O A
D T N E G I C O M D N D
E H C H X S C H I O O R
M E G A C L I T E M E A
Y A R R L A N R D E D S
N P N P O L O O E T N T
A E B A E K I S O N O E
G L K L I L O S A N P A
P A P Y G T H I T D S H
A R H K L S N A H O H P
S A O E I A Y E E D E I
I E B N L G K U B M R S
T N O T E I R H E E M A
H P S T S O K N R U I P
E N E C P C M E I T P H
E K N A N A E M N M P O
O N A R N S D R O T E H
E T R P U T T A M H B U
T H Y O N E D C E D H A
```

Answer on page 178.

37. OPI LOVE U

Find all the OPI nail polish colors hiding in the grid. The leftover letters spell a quote and its speaker.

ALTAR EGO

BASTILLE MY HEART

BERLIN [THERE DONE THAT]

BLUE [MY MIND]

CAJUN SHRIMP

CUTE LITTLE VIXEN

FIRST DATE [AT THE GOLDEN GATE]

[FLASHBULB] FUCHSIA

GLITZERLAND

[I REACHED MY] GOLD!

HEY BABY

[YOU DON'T KNOW] JACQUES!

JINX

MIAMI BEET

MIDNIGHT [IN MOSCOW]

[ATOMIC] ORANGE

PASSION

ROSY FUTURE

[LIGHT MY] SAPPHIRE

SOLITAIRE

SPRUNG

SWEET HEART

TEAL [THE COWS COME HOME]

TIFFANY CASE

VESPER

```
L U T R A E H T E E W S
C K E P A S S I O N C O
N S E M I S T F D S L A
R G B I E L U Y N C O F
V H I R A C B N A U G E
E I M H H N A E L T G S
S O A S X G S N R E B A
P Y I N N Y T O E L M C
E A M U I U I D Z I I Y
R R R J J F L I T T D N
O P N A G O L S I T N A
S R E C G R E O L L I F
Y A A N A I M L G E G F
F L P N S U Y I N V H I
U I T P G I H T L I T T
T S R B H E E A T X H I
U E L S N I A I G E S S
R U A T T A R R R N T T
E Q E O G D T E O Y O U
R C T A L T A R E G O W
A A Y A A R O T N A L L
S J T Y B A B Y E H O N
```

38. AUTOBOTS

Find all the Transformers hiding in the grid.
The leftover letters spell a quote and its speaker.

BEACHCOMBER
BLASTER
BLURR
BRAWN
BUMPER
CLIFFJUMPER
EJECT
GEARS
GRAPPLE
GRIMLOCK
HOIST
HOT ROD
HUBCAP
INFERNO
JAZZ
KUP
MIRAGE
OUTBACK
PERCEPTOR
PIPES
PROWL
PUNCH
RATCHET
RED ALERT
REWIND
SKIDS
SLAG
SMOKESCREEN
SNARL
STEELJAW
SUNSTREAKER
SWERVE
SWOOP
TOPSPIN
TRACKS
TRAILBREAKER
WARPATH
WHIRL
WINDCHARGER

F B U M P E R E W I N D
R E B M O C H C A E B O
R S U N S T R E A K E R
E E D O A M P J I S B T
R O T P E C R E P T R O
J G R I M L O C K A A H
P A C B U H W T I H W R
W L Z E T H L L S R N A
I S I Z I R B R G I H T
N T O R L R A N S I O C
D E L F E E S C N A S H
C L E A G M W F K L T E
H L K R I S E E C S E T
A E I R C R R N A K E T
R I A F N S V E B I L B
G G N O F K E L T D J L
E R N I T J U K U S A A
R A B E P R U P O O W S
I P N G R S S M U M O T
P P T I S E P I P N S E
M L U S P R I O M E C R
R E D A L E R T T E R H

39. DECEPTICONS

Find all the Transformers hiding in the grid.
The leftover letters spell a quote and its speaker.

BARRAGE

BLAST OFF

BLOT

BOMBSHELL

BONECRUSHER

DEAD END

DIVEBOMB

DRAG STRIP

HEADSTRONG

HOOK

LASERBEAK

LONG HAUL

MOTORMASTER

OCTANE

ONSLAUGHT

OVERBITE

OVERKILL

POUNCE

RANSACK

RATBAT

RAVAGE

RAZORCLAW

RUCKUS

RUMBLE

SCOURGE

SCRAPPER

SHRAPNEL

SKALOR

SOUNDWAVE

STARSCREAM

SWINDLE

VENOM

VORTEX

WILDRIDER

```
Y O U S E G A R R A B T
T R E T S A M R O T O M
I O L T H G U A L S N O
L L L W I L D R I D E R
K A E B R E S A L T C F
C K W A L C R O Z A R I
A S G H H A T F D B U O
S M A E R C S R A T S S
N O R A T A A T H A H W
A V E D E G V X O R E I
R E W S S T E A A F R N
R R G T O T I P G U F D
E K R R R U N B C E E L
P I E O U E N K R A E E
P L V N L O U D D E A B
A L O G A S C E W R V M
R K T N H T N S U A A O
C T I S G D C M W H V B
S Y K O O H B O Y O E E
U L O S E L A M E G N V
A T R O E C N U O P O I
N B O M B S H E L L M D
```

Answer on page 179.

40. DEWEY DECIMAL SYSTEM

Find all the Dewey Decimal System–related answers hiding in the grid. The leftover letters spell a quote and its speaker.

ALGEBRA

ANALOGY

ARTS

AVES

BIBLE

BIBLIOGRAPHY

BOTANY

CHANGE

COLOR

CUSTOMS

DATA
  PROCESSING

DRAMA

DREAMS

ECOLOGY

ETHICS

FICTION

FISH

FRENCH

FRUITS

GLASS

GREEK

HEAT

HISTORY

INSURANCE

LEGEND

LOGIC

MINING

MUSIC

PHYSICS

PRINTS

PSYCHOLOGY

RARE BOOKS

RELIGION

SECTS

SPACE

SYSTEMS

TIME

ZOOLOGY

```
F R E N C H H K E U S M
A I Y G O L O C E Y A N
B V S P R I N T S E E H
A V E H S A T T G I R O
N R M S R F E C N L O G
O W A U C M S T I U R F
I L S I S S T Y S F F R
G N G P O I G M S L T H
I O A H M O C S E R Y A
L C E E L E E G C G M M
E G N A H C E A O A I Y
R T N T T N S L R N H S
O A H S D M O D P P U R
C E R I A H A S A D Y S
H E S E C R I R T N R C
E I R Y B S G E A M O I
T D S E I O M T D O N S
E P G T I Z O O L O G Y
A L N L O B D K T K N H
A O B W A R T S S S L P
M I N I N G Y E D G U E
B P L A B T O R O L O C
```

41. "THE SIMPSONS"

Find all the character names hiding
in the grid. The leftover letters spell
a quote spoken by Grampa Simpson.

APU	LIONEL HUTZ
ARTIE ZIFF	LISA
BARNEY	LURLEEN
BART	MAGGIE
BLINKY	MARGE
CARL	MARTIN
CLETUS	MAYOR QUIMBY
COMIC BOOK GUY	MILHOUSE
DR. NICK	MOE
DUFFMAN	MR. BURNS
FAT TONY	NED FLANDERS
HOMER	NELSON
ITCHY	PATTY
JIMBO	RALPH
KANG	SCRATCHY
KENT BROCKMAN	SELMA
KODOS	SKINNER
KRUSTY	ÜTER
LENNY	WILLIE

```
S F A T T O N Y I U S Z
E C D D A M L E S T T O
B M R B U R N S L U E B
I W I A L F T H H S I L
T T G E T B F L U R O I
C T N I T C E M H E E N
H N A L N N H G A D T K
Y Y K L O A H Y R N H Y
U B E I Y M C N H A O T
G M L W H K I A P L M T
K I U N G C B E L F E A
O U R D K O N A A D R P
O Q L A W R H I R E A T
B R E P R B I E T N T W
C O E U A T N C S R E A
I Y N N J N I L A D A Y
M A G G I E N E O R W M
O M W K M K H T Z A L O
C T S O B I A U R I M E
W I T D O H S S T A F I
E S U O H L I M S E B F
K R U S T Y L N T I R T
```

42. COME RIGHT IN, SIT RIGHT DOWN

Find all the restaurants hiding in the grid. The leftover letters spell a quote and its speaker.

APPLEBEE'S

BENNIGAN'S

BOB EVANS

BUFFALO WILD
  WINGS

CARRABBA'S

CHEDDAR'S

CHEVYS

CHILI'S

CRACKER BARREL

DENNY'S

ELEPHANT BAR

FRIENDLY'S

FUDDRUCKERS

HARD ROCK CAFE

HOULIHAN'S

[THE] MELTING POT

OLIVE GARDEN

PERKINS

P.F. CHANG'S

RED ROBIN

STEAK 'N SHAKE

TGI FRIDAYS

```
T O P G N I T L E M I H
M N E D R A G E V I L O
P L A G P U I L L E D U
W I T H F I F E E N S L
D D E C C I R P R S N I
B I E O H N I H R I A H
U N M N A Y D A A L G A
F S I F N E A N B E I N
F R R I G Y Y T R F N S
A C I A S A S B E A N N
L P T E D F I A K C E G
O E P U N D R R C K B F
W R E L O D E U A C T U
I K W H E D L H R O A D
L I T T R B S Y C R O D
D N O O R N E D S D E R
W S B R K I N E S R A U
I I R A E S T Y S A A C
N U E R A N V T C H H K
G T B O B E V A N S U E
S C K C H I L I S C L R
O S E C A R R A B B A S
```

43. TALKIN' TOLKIEN

Find all the character names hiding in the grid. The leftover letters spell a quote from "The Lord of the Rings."

ARAGORN

ARWEN

BARLIMAN

BILBO

BOROMIR

CELEBORN

DENETHOR

DÉORWINE

DERVORIN

ELROND

ÉOWYN

FARAMIR

GALADRIEL

GANDALF THE
  GREY

GIMLI

GOLLUM

GRÍMA

HIRLUIN

ISILDUR

LEGOLAS

MERRY

PIPPIN

SAMWISE
  GAMGEE

SARUMAN

SAURON

SHELOB

SMAUG

THÉODEN

THRANDUIL

TREEBEARD

```
O N S E R N I U L R I H
S M A U G B I E N M G T
A O U T A R I I R U U L
M E R H N R I L T L H E
W M O R D L A M B L L L
I O N A A E E I A O N B
S E L N L O N G R G I O
E A N D F W I E O G T L
G R O U T Y P F T L I E
A A N I H N P D T H A H
M G D L E H I E M O O S
G O N E G E P R I N A R
E R B O R O M I R R G T
E N O B E V R I U N D T
N L A G Y T O M D H R H
I R R M E M A R L A A E
W I O O I N L L I A E O
R M N B N L D I S N B D
O A E N E D R T I H E E
E R E R D L A A R W E N
D A R K R N E E B S R S
B F I N D Y T C H E T M
```

Answer on page 180.

44. A BONE TO PICK

Find all the bone-related words hiding in the grid.
The leftover letters spell a quote and its speaker.

ANKLE
CLAVICLE
COCCYX
CUBOID
FEMUR
FIBULA
HUMERUS
LUMBAR
MALLEUS
MANDIBLE
MAXILLA
METACARPAL
METATARSAL
OCCIPITAL

PATELLA
PHALANGES
RADIUS
RIBS
SACRUM
SCAPULA
STERNUM
TALUS
TEMPORAL
THORACIC
TIBIA
TRAPEZIUM
ULNA

```
A N O O S N E S W I T L
I N L U S E V U E R H K
B N L A T I P I C C O O
I A A U E W W D H A R T
T L P I R N C A O L A D
B L R L N O O R D T C O
O E A C U B O I D O I K
M T C R M O U T C O C F
U A A M O E I C T R S C
I P T R A P Y P A E D M
Z E E R I X M B F G H T
E D M A H U M E R U S O
P L W A L U M L T N T O
A T C H L U E K M A F R
R L R I R L P N M I O W
T O L F V M E A B Y B S
O N E I S A N U C I T A
N R E A X D L R S S L C
Y K I I I A L C L E D R
M E T B R U M M A N C U
A P L A S R A T A T E M
S E G N A L A H P O T E
```

Answer on page 180.

45. ASTRONAUTS T-Z

Find all the astronauts hiding in the grid.
The leftover letters spell a quote by Sally Ride.

TANI

TANNER

THAGARD

THOMAS

THORNE

THORNTON

THUOT

TRINH

TRULY

VAN DEN BERG

VAN HOFTEN

VEACH

VOSS

WALKER

WALZ

WANG

WEBER

WEITZ

WETHERBEE

WHITE

WILLIAMS

WISOFF

WOLF

WOODWARD

WORDEN

YOUNG

ZAMKA

```
T H A G A R D T G F O R
W H C A E V W O R D E N
H A A K M A Z T E U E V
E R L R E A S O B N L I
D A I W D N T S N U C Y
W E T H E R B E E C U O
I E M I B T G E D Z O U
S T B T H E S N N L T N
O E R E E O O R A A T G
F Y P E R T T O V W H A
F T S C N E I H E N C E
W L A R S N N T A N I T
N F O O R G H N I R L S
E H I W N O E V A E R W
T R A N M I N T O T O A
F T E A A C H E R O O R
O A S C O U N S D U E L
H O R S Z W H W O H T O
N L S D M T A E T T H A
A O T S T R I N H C I E
V N C E D W A E S F O R
B S M A I L L I W O Y S
```

46. HORROR MOVIES

Find all the movies hiding in the grid. The leftover letters spell a quote from "Scream."

[THE] ADDICTION
ALIENS
[THE] BIRDS
CARRIE
DON'T LOOK NOW
[THE] EVIL DEAD
[THE] EXORCIST
FRANKENSTEIN
GREMLINS
HALLOWEEN
[THE] HOWLING
JAWS
NEAR DARK
[A] NIGHTMARE ON
  ELM STREET

NOSFERATU
[THE] OMEN
[THE] OTHERS
POLTERGEIST
PSYCHO
REPULSION
[THE] RING
ROSEMARY'S BABY
[THE] SHINING
[THE] SILENCE OF
  THE LAMBS

[THE] WICKER MAN

```
T N O I S L U P E R H E
F R E A D R E C E R T A
K R A D R A E N G N L D
A O A O I S I N N I R D
N S U N B I I L E G E I
A E S T K L T N H H A C
M M M L W E S T P T G T
R A O O N N N E O M R I
E R H O M C O S L A E O
K Y U K S E S W T R M N
C S T N A O F A E E L B
I B I O D F E J R O I G
W A E W B T R D G N N N
Y B G H I H A N E E S I
O Y N R A E T D I L E R
R T I O D L U S S M P U
C C N L E A L S T S S E
F U I L L M Y O Y T I S
U V H R V B I C W R V E
E A S H O S H R R E R O
S R E H T O R A M E E O
V I E X O R C I S T E N
```

47. SPANISH 101

Find all the Spanish words hiding in the grid. The leftover letters spell a quote by Salma Hayek.

ABRIL	CUATRO	MARZO
ABUELA	DIEZ	MIÉRCOLES
AGOSTO	DOMINGO	NEGRO
AGUA	ENERO	NOCHE
AMARILLO	FÁCIL	OCHO
ANARAN-JADO	FRÍO	PADRE
	GATO	POLLO
ARROZ	GRIS	RICO
AZUL	HERMANA	ROJO
BLANCO	HERMANO	ROSADO
BUENO	JULIO	SÁBADO
BURRO	JUNIO	SEIS
CABEZA	LECHE	TARDE
CALIENTE	LUNES	TORO
CAMISA	MADRE	TRES
CARNE	MAÑANA	VACA
CORAZÓN	MARTES	VERDE

```
M Y O D R I D V O J O R
C M A R T E S I U I N P
G A A S T B A L E U B A
I D M E L A I L I Z O D
T R I I E O U I S O T R
F E O S S R N C D O S E
O M D A N A N A M C O O
B L A N C O J F M I G H
O M S E Z N C E N R A C
X I O A A I T H H S E O
C O R R L H O E E E A H
V O A F U E R L D N H E
C N L C Z M O R R U B P
A A U G A C E I S L E D
L M B N R V M I N E B G
I E A E A R R O Z U A T
E T I R Z G S G E B J H
N M R O I A U N R G O E
T R E S B L O I H L H H
E D R A T T L M L O L C
L Y D M A R Z O R E N E
W O R G E N P D O O D L
```

48. SHAKESPEARE CHARACTERS

Find all the characters hiding in the grid. The leftover letters spell a quote from "As You Like It."

ACHILLES
ADRIAN
AGRIPPA
ARIEL
BAGOT
BANQUO
BATES
BENEDICK
BIANCA
CASCA
CERES
CLAUDIUS
CORDELIA
CYMBELINE
DESDEMONA
DOGBERRY
DUNCAN
ESCALUS
FESTE
GERTRUDE
GONERIL

GRUMIO
HOTSPUR
IAGO
IRIS
JULIET
JUNO
LENNOX
LORENZO
MACDUFF
MOTH
OBERON
ORSINO
OSRIC
POLONIUS
PUCK
SALERIO
SEXTON
SNOUT
TITUS
VERGES
VIOLA

```
T  H  J  E  P  O  L  O  N  I  U  S
E  D  U  R  T  R  E  G  F  O  N  E
O  L  L  D  S  O  M  T  S  A  H  R
T  V  I  O  L  A  O  U  I  H  U  E
I  N  E  K  C  U  L  R  H  P  E  C
I  S  T  D  Q  A  D  E  S  W  I  O
S  D  U  N  C  A  N  T  R  L  E  R
B  F  A  S  C  F  O  I  U  I  T  D
F  B  E  S  E  H  K  T  T  R  O  E
H  E  A  S  U  W  C  U  I  E  S  L
E  C  T  T  M  I  I  S  A  N  N  I
T  E  O  D  E  S  D  E  M  O  N  A
O  N  I  K  N  S  E  U  O  G  T  G
G  I  M  W  S  L  N  S  A  U  H  O
A  L  U  O  Z  N  E  R  O  L  K  I
B  E  R  S  T  L  B  N  E  N  C  M
I  B  G  R  L  H  S  I  N  S  U  E
A  M  L  I  N  O  R  E  B  O  P  J
N  Y  H  C  F  A  T  O  G  I  X  B
C  C  E  A  D  O  G  B  E  R  R  Y
A  G  R  I  P  P  A  F  O  I  E  O
O  R  S  I  N  O  T  X  E  S  L  V
```

Answer on page 181.

49. "DOCTOR WHO" COMPANIONS

Find all the companions hiding in the grid.
The leftover letters spell a quote
spoken by the Eleventh Doctor.

ADRIC

AMY POND

BARBARA WRIGHT

BEN JACKSON

CLARA OSWALD

GRACE HOLLOWAY

HARRY SULLIVAN

JACK HARKNESS

JACKSON LAKE

JAMIE MCCRIMMON

JO GRANT

KAMELION

KATARINA

LEELA

LIZ SHAW

MELANIE BUSH

NYSSA

POLLY

ROMANA

VICKI

VICTORIA
WATERFIELD

VISLOR TURLOUGH

```
D N O P Y M A N V L E V
N O I L E M A K I E R I
G N L E E L A Z C N O R
E O C O A S S V T N I N
P M C D S H I I O A D E
N M R Y A C E S R V U N
L I N W G E K L I I S S
C R O F R C V O A L C O
U C R S A I E R W L Y O
H C U J C R E T A U T B
S M N K E U S U T S H S
U E I C H Y I R E Y G S
B I K L O N W L R R I E
E M A A L H I O F R R N
I A T R L C H U I A W K
N J A A O N C G E H A R
A O R O W M O H L A R A
L G I S A S A S D E A H
E R N W Y A L N K W B K
M A A A A Y S I A C R C
G N N L O R E C O I A A
N T C D I D E N C E B J
```

50. WORDS TO MAKE YOU SOUND SMART

Find all the vocabulary words hiding in the grid.
The leftover letters spell a quote and its speaker.

ACCOLADE

ANGST

ANTIDOTE

BAROQUE

BOONDOGGLE

BROGUE

CAMARADERIE

CHARISMA

DILETTANTE

ÉLAN

ENNUI

EPITOME

EQUIVOCATE

FIASCO

GLIB

HEDONIST

IDYLLIC

KITSCH

LURID

MANTRA

MAUDLIN

NARCISSIST

NIRVANA

OGLE

PANACEA

PEEVISH

PRECOCIOUS

REVEL

RHETORIC

STOIC

SUAVE

TRYST

UBIQUITOUS

VILE

WAFT

ZEALOUS

```
M Y R C H A R I S M A M
A N H A E C A N A P E T
R A E C L T S Y R T M I
E S T I G R N T V E O A
D L O L O C S A I F T E
A I R L D I R U L K I L
L Z I Y H S I V E E P G
O E C D T Y A O T E E G
C U R I E F G N T O M O
C I N U O G A A G A A D
A P T N O T C W U S N N
M F R N T O S D H A T O
A U R E V E L E I L R O
R B L I C I D A L L A B
A I U A N O T H E T A I
D Q N M N E C A N R E D
E U A I C T C I O E V P
R I S T R B I Q O I A T
I T M A I V U D R U U K
E O B L Z E A L O U S U
E U G O R B R N N T E T
T S I S S I C R A N E T
```

51. EPONYMS A-K

Find all the eponyms hiding in the grid.
The leftover letters spell a quote and its speaker.

ACHILLES

ALZHEIMER

AMPÈRE

ÅNGSTRÖM

APGAR

ATKINS

BEAUFORT

BECK

BELL

BERING

BOSE

BOWIE

BOYCOTT

BOYLE

BUICK

BUNSEN

CASANOVA

CELSIUS

CESSNA

CHEVROLET

CHRYSLER

COLT

DELL

DEWEY

DIESEL

DOLBY

FAHRENHEIT

FERRARI

FORBES

FORD

GLOCK

GRAHAM

HEIMLICH

HEINEKEN

HERSHEY

HERTZ

HONDA

HOOVER

JACUZZI

JOULE

KELVIN

```
J O U L E L Y O B W H E
N Y H E I N E K E N B O
S E L L I H C A C U O J
H C I L M I E H K W Y A
A A A N U O R S E T C C
F S L B D T R A O R O U
O A Z F E E O T R B T Z
F N H O L L W F S R T Z
O O E R L L L E O G E I
R V I L E T H E Y R N F
B A M S W N C O R A D A
E R E P M A H H L H O T
S I R D T O E E N A L K
D E I W O B V R I M B I
B C E V U L R S V T Y N
E L E N T A O H L H E S
R R S S G H L E E T R U
I E U P S O E Y K T H I
N O A T T N T L O C O S
G L O C K D A V O N B L
T R O F U A E B I S M E
A R C K R E L S Y R H C
```

Answer on page 182.

52. EPONYMS L-W

Find all the eponyms hiding in the grid. The leftover letters spell a quote and its speaker.

LÉOTARD

LUTZ

MACH

MANDELBROT

MASON

MCDONALD

MELBA

MILQUETOAST

MOOG

MORSE

MURPHY

NEHRU

NESTLÉ

NEWTON

NOBEL

OHM

OORT

PARKINSON

PASCAL

PASTEUR

PAVLOV

PENNEY

PONZI

PORSCHE

REUTER

RUBIK

SALCHOW

SAX

SEARS

SHRAPNEL

[DE] SILHOUETTE

SINGER

STRAUSS

[SHIRLEY] TEMPLE

TURING

VENN

VOLTA

WATT

WINCHESTER

```
I D L E N P A R H S O N
P T A S T R A U S S C A
E H C S R O P R E T H A
N T S E M A C H T H E E
N Y A T S S E D T O L S
E L P T E M L S Y P I R
Y D E E E A V A M I E O
C U N U N O B E L G W M
R A R O O E T E N A T H
A T D H S T W I T N H K
E C Y L A N S T D O I N
M T T I M H I L O B A V
I U O S A X T K U N E D
L A R E U T E R R T R N
Q Y B P R O L F O A Z T
U S L H H E T I T O P R
E A E O E Y S O W O A N
T L D N N G E I N K V O
O C N L O L N Z A T L E
A H A O G N I R U T O S
S O M E L B A T L O V L
T W I N C H E S T E R A
```

53. GEOLOGY WHIZ

Find all the geological terms hiding in the grid.
The leftover letters spell a quote by Kathy B. Steele.

ACREAGE

ARROYO

ATOLL

BASIN

BAUXITE

BEDROCK

BITUMINOUS

BUTTE

CLAY

DELTA

DUNE

EROSION

FAULT

FJORD

FLOOD PLAIN

FOSSIL

GEYSER

GLACIER

IGNEOUS

MAGMA

MANTLE

METAMORPHIC

MINERAL

PLATEAU

QUARTZ

RESERVOIR

SEDIMENTARY

SINKHOLE

VOLCANO

```
B I T U M I N O U S Z I
U M W E A U I N T I T N
T T E A G L A C I E R O
T D G T M E L E O L A O
E G E O A Y P B T E U C
A U C L S M D E I A Q L
F A U L T I O K E B L E
I N R A A A O R G O U P
F J O R D Y L E P T D O
O R E E O S F S A H N D
B E L N C Y N E A U I S
E E I I U O O R V E R C
Y B S M I D O V O D Y S
E E S S M E D O N L I K
E F O R E E E I A S S P
I R F R I G S R C T I I
E T I X U A B S L O N G
R R E N B E D R O C K N
G E Y S E R E G V A H E
D E S O R C S O M E O O
T H I N M A N T L E L U
G Y R A T N E M I D E S
```

54. STATE MOTTOS

Find all the motto words hiding in the grid. The leftover letters spell a quote and its speaker.

BREATHE	PEACE
CONQUERS	PEOPLE
CROSSROADS	PRIZE
DEEDS	PROSPERITY
DEFEND	RIGHTS
DIRECT	RULE
ENRICHES	SEEM
EQUALITY	SILVER
FOUND	SUSTAINS
FREE	TRANSPLANTED
FUTURE	TRUST
GOES	TYRANTS
GROWS	UNITY
HOPE	UPWARD
INDUSTRY	VALOR
JUSTICE	VIRTUE
LABOR	WELFARE
LIBERTY	WINGS
NORTH	WISDOM

```
T H I S B R P C E C S E
F U T U R E R R U L E A
M E A C O V O O I R E J
P R E P I L S S F Z M U
E D L R A I P S G O E S
A E T V O S E R O F D T
C U M I G H R O N E R I
E E D N C A I A E A N C
L T I I T E T D N D M E
I W R P T N Y S U T H H
B N E E O T P S U I M T
E P C R I L T O S R S A
R S T N A R Y T I B T E
T H U N Y L E L A B O R
Y I T N O R D E R T I B
O E Q U A L I T Y G I M
D N U O F P R O H R V E
E R A F L E W T Y O O U
F R A M O D S I W W W O
E R K W S N I A T S U S
N B E E P O H T T E D A
D C O N Q U E R S V I S
```

Answer on page 183.

55. I'M NUMBER ONE: 2000s

Find all the recording artists hiding in the grid.
The leftover letters spell a quote by Lady Gaga.

AKON

ALICIA KEYS

ASHANTI

CIARA

CLAY AIKEN

CRAZY TOWN

CREED

EMINEM

FANTASIA

FERGIE

FLO RIDA

JANET [JACKSON]

JA RULE

JASON DERULO

JAY-Z

LADY GAGA

LONESTAR

LUDACRIS

MARIO

MARY J. BLIGE

MIMS

NELLY

*NSYNC

OWL CITY

PINK

RIHANNA

SEAN PAUL

SHAGGY

SHAKIRA

SISQÓ

TERROR SQUAD

T-PAIN

TWISTA

USHER

VERTICAL HORIZON

```
T W H N E U F T H F E S
R E O I S L M W A N E Y
A K R H O R I N N O G E
A L E R O T T S O Z M K
S R I F O A M A K I E A
H D A R S R U P N R O I
A T S I W T S E R O N C
N E A H C C M Q O H M I
T N S A E R A K U L E L
I A M N L A D Y G A G A
U J I N U Z P I M C D N
A J M A R Y J B L I G E
Z Y A J A T L W A T Y K
S S T S J O D E E R C I
I M H E O W W S A E M A
R A T S E N O L E V R Y
C R P H I E D E C I R A
A I S A G L O E K I C L
D O P G R L N A R N T C
U T I G E Y H I Y U N Y
L S N Y F S I S Q O L I
D E K S E A N P A U L O
```

56. STEPHEN KING CHARACTERS

Find all the characters hiding in the grid. The leftover letters spell a quote by Stephen King.

BARLOW
BATEMAN
BEAUMONT
CHAMBERS
CLAIBORNE
COFFEY
COSLAW
CRANDALL
CREED
CULLEN
CUNNINGHAM
DARNELL
DESCHAIN
DESJARDIN
EDGECOMBE
FLAGG
GAUNT

HALLORANN
HANSCOM
KASPBRAK
LOWE
MCGEE
MEARS
REPPERTON
ROBERTS
RUSK
SHELDON
SMITH
STARK
STILLSON
TRENTON
WHITE
WILKES

```
K A S P B R A K Y M O B
U S T R E B O R A S C E
A N I R A N Y H O H T A
H O L R E E G P B E E U
T O L S F N W A B L E M
E O S F I P T M S D O O
W M O N E E O O E O O N
N C N E M C E S N N I T
L U S A E E J A W A C A
C L N G C A L Y H R B Y
K L D T R L H C A E M F
R E O D E R S N E O C E
A N I N E E D N C O F Y
T N R F D A R S C O U R
S A W R L O N O H I T I
D R N L B A S E A G U N
T O A I H L G E M I L I
T L A E A T T G B G H A
S L B W M I I C E A E E
C A O N H D O M R U S K
N H E W I L K E S N T O
Y O U R E P P E R T O N
```

57. HAPPY EARTH DAY

Find all the Earth-related words and phrases hiding in the grid. The leftover letters spell a quote and its speaker.

AFRICA
ARCTIC
ASIA
ATLANTIC
AUSTRALIA
AXIS
CENTRAL AMERICA
DEGREES
EQUATOR
EQUINOX
EUROPE
HEMISPHERE
INDIAN

LATITUDE
LONGITUDE
MIDDLE EAST
NORTH AMERICA
NORTH POLE
OZONE
PACIFIC
PRIME MERIDIAN
SEA LEVEL
SOUTH AMERICA
SOUTH POLE
TIDES

```
M I D D L E E A S T F O
A R G S E T D E N L O T
I T I H A E D T T E A H
L X E E G I A R T V C H
A N O R T H P O L E I P
R R E D U T I T A L R R
T E C I T N A L T A E I
S O U T H P O L E E M M
U O D E I L I G H S A E
A T U P A C I F I C L M
S C T T O F E A I S A E
E L I Y H O U R B E R R
A R E R F A E E R T T I
A N L D E T M E H E N D
X W I O N M H E D S E I
L O O N N P A F R I C A
G T N O S G P H O I L N
A N A I D N I Y T W C I
T H M Y U O U T A R R A
H E A I R Q K A U H O L
H E P O R U E I Q D L N
G I B R O Z O N E A E N
```

58. ROM-COMS

Find all the romantic comedies hiding in the grid.
The leftover letters spell a quote and its source.

ABOUT LAST NIGHT

ANNIE HALL

AS GOOD AS IT GETS

BREAKFAST [AT TIFFANY'S]

[THE] BREAK-UP

[THE SHOP AROUND THE] CORNER

[50] FIRST DATES

FOUR [WEDDINGS AND A FUNERAL]

GREEN CARD

[NOTTING] HILL

IRMA [LA DOUCE]

[THE SEVEN YEAR] ITCH

[CITY] LIGHTS

MAID [IN MANHATTAN]

MIGHTY [APHRODITE]

MOONSTRUCK

NEW YEAR'S EVE

ONE FINE DAY

PILLOW [TALK]

PRETTY WOMAN

RUNAWAY [BRIDE]

[WHEN HARRY MET] SALLY ...

SHE'S ALL THAT

[THE WEDDING] SINGER

[WHILE YOU WERE] SLEEPING

[THE PHILADELPHIA] STORY

VALENTINE'S DAY

[WHAT WOMEN] WANT

[MY BEST FRIEND'S] WEDDING

```
T A H T L L A S E H S P
T H E C I L A T T W R I
H I N G T L G E A E B L
O U H T L I R G T D O L
M T A Y R H S T N D P O
S C R M A E Y I G I U W
E I A U B W A S N N K S
T P E O O P D A I G A L
A N V M U F E D P E E O
D A A N T L N O E Y R R
T N L W L G I O E N B U
S N E E A T F G L E K N
R I N T S O E S S W C A
I E T G T T N A E Y U W
F H I T N C O R N E R A
H A N E I R R R I A T Y
G L E H G T A T Y R S T
H L S E H V E R Y S N E
N D D M T L O V E E O A
T S A F K A E R B V O C
T I Y T H G I M U E M A
D R A C N E E R G L L Y
```

Answer on page 184.

59. TIME'S MOST INFLUENTIAL MEN (2014)

Find all the men hiding in the grid. The leftover letters spell a quote by Benedict Cumberbatch.

AL-KADDRI
AL-SISI
BEZOS
BROWN
COLLINS
CUARÓN
CUMBERBATCH
DANGOTE
FADELL
FRANCIS
GREEN
HALDANE
HOLDER
ICAHN
JINPING
KALANICK
KEJRIWAL
KERRY
KOCH
KOVAC
LANZA
LAYAMA

LOPEZ
MADURO
MCCONAUGHEY
MCMASTER
MCQUEEN
MEYERS
MODI
MUJICA
MURPHY
OBAMA
PEELE
RAHMAN
RONALDO
ROSE
SHERMAN
SINCLAIR
SNOWDEN
SPIEGEL
STEYER
WAINAINA
WALKER
WILLIAMS

```
E I R D D A K L A N J O
Y T M C M A S T E R Z H
R F R A N C I S O E O E
I R Y B E Z O S P J B O
A A H M D U E O R N A E
L H C C W I L L I A M S
C M T C O R U D A M A D
N A A O N K E Y E O Z A
I N B N S E O Y O D N N
S F R A L J E V E I A G
C I E U F R E U A T L O
U H B G S I J N Q C S T
A O M H A W I W N C D E
R L U E N A N O O T M N
O D C Y W L P R J U K A
N E O R A E I B S T C D
A R L R L G N H A C I L
L C L E K E G R E E N A
D T I K E I S I S L A H
O H N J R P F A D E L L
E E S N U S H E R M A N
Y H P R U M D G A M K E
```

60. TIME'S MOST INFLUENTIAL WOMEN (2014)

Find all the women hiding in the grid. The leftover letters spell a quote by Malala Yousafzai.

ABRAMOVIC	MASSENET
ADAMS	MERKEL
ADMATI	OKOLLOH
AL-THANI	OKONJO-IWEALA
ANDERSON-LOPEZ	PAULUS
BACHELET	PETTIGREW
BARRA	PHILO
BEYONCÉ	SULISTYANINGSIH
BURNS	SULLIVAN
CHEN	TARTT
CLINTON	TAYLOR
COUSIN	UNDERWOOD
CYRUS	WATERS
ELLISON	WHITE
GILLIBRAND	WILLIAMS
HAYHOE	WRIGHT
KELLY	YELLEN
KOHAN	YOUSAFZAI

```
W  H  B  E  Y  O  N  C  E  P  E  H
T  A  Y  L  O  R  N  A  H  N  N  A
T  T  H  D  E  I  W  I  H  O  H  Y
B  O  R  N  T  L  L  E  S  O  O  H
A  B  R  A  M  O  V  I  C  U  K  O
R  W  M  R  T  O  L  R  S  N  O  E
R  D  L  B  D  L  I  A  U  D  N  C
A  Y  W  I  E  S  F  N  L  E  J  Y
D  W  E  L  S  Z  I  D  I  R  O  R
A  H  R  L  A  L  C  E  S  W  I  U
M  I  G  I  L  E  L  R  T  O  W  S
S  T  I  G  G  E  I  S  Y  O  E  N
N  E  T  T  E  H  N  O  A  D  A  R
W  A  T  E  R  S  T  N  N  V  L  U
P  E  E  B  N  O  O  L  I  N  A  B
A  E  P  A  V  O  N  O  N  M  L  I
U  C  E  C  B  E  K  P  G  E  T  C
L  O  M  H  K  O  E  E  S  R  H  S
U  P  O  E  L  W  E  Z  I  K  A  C
S  U  L  L  I  V  A  N  H  E  N  R
F  L  O  E  S  M  A  I  L  L  I  W
Y  H  U  T  E  N  E  S  S  A  M  L
```

Answer on page 184.

61. STUDY HAUL

Find all the fields of study hiding in the grid. The leftover letters spell a quote by Wernher von Braun.

ANATOMY

ARCHAEOLOGY

BIOLOGY

BIOPHYSICS

BOTANY

CRYSTALLOGRAPHY

ECOLOGY

ENDOCRINOLOGY

ENTOMOLOGY

FORESTRY

GENETICS

GEOGRAPHY

GEOLOGY

HEMATOLOGY

HYDROLOGY

ICHTHYOLOGY

METROLOGY

NEUROLOGY

OCEANOGRAPHY

ONCOLOGY

OPTICS

PETROLOGY

PHYSIOLOGY

PSYCHOLOGY

ROBOTICS

SEISMOLOGY

TAXONOMY

```
P E T R O L O G Y B A S
I N C Y R Y E Y S Y Y E
A D Y R G G C G G H G R
S O H Y G O L O C E O O
E C P I G L L L S W L B
I R A H A O T O I A O O
S I R M C Y L M I O I T
M N G N D H O O P B S I
O O O I N T G T E W Y C
L L L H E H I N N G H S
O O L I D C O E O E P C
G G A P S I F L C O N I
Y Y T S T M O K E G N S
G G S Y T E R S A R O Y
O O Y C A T E C N A A H
L L R H X R S I O P N P
O O C O O O T T G H A O
T R W L N L R E R Y T I
A U W O O O Y N A T O B
M E H G M G A E P T M I
E N A Y Y Y M G H D Y O
H Y D R O L O G Y I N G
```

62. MY LITTLE PONY

Find all the ponies hiding in the grid. The leftover letters spell a quote spoken by Pinkie Pie.

BABY BOUNCY
BRIGHTGLOW
CLOUD CLIMBER
COCONUT GROVE
COTTON CANDY
DANGLES
DERPY
FIREFLY
FIZZY
GALAXY
GLORY
HEART THROB
ISLAND DELIGHT
LIGHTNING [DUST]
LOCKET
MIMIC
MINTY

PARADISE
POSEY
RARITY
SHAGGY
SOARIN
SPARKLEWORKS
SPITFIRE
SQUIRMY
SUNNY DAZE
SWEETBERRY
TAPPY
TRIXIE [LULAMOON]
TWILIGHT [SPARKLE]
WHIZZER
WYSTERIA
YO-YO

```
R I B T A P P Y L L I S
A E A E R E Z Z I H W Y
R K B E R Z F G U E O D
I N Y M I I H N E Y H N
T Y B F I T F T O E W A
Y S O O N L B T A S W C
T H U I R E C R I O D N
H A N S R M T D L P O O
G G C R N T I G U E S T
I G Y O H F T M M O Y T
L Y F R A H V O I R L O
E V O R G T U N O C O C
D B M I N T Y X A L A G
D E R P Y M R I U Q S L
N B I E I X I R T T E O
A I R E T S Y W F U N R
L O C K E T I N S Y W Y
S P A R K L E W O R K S
I O E S I D A R A P R D
S E L G N A D S R I S K
U M H Y L F E R I F Q U
A T E Z A D Y N N U S T
```

63. 5-LETTER SCRABBLE WORDS

Find all the Scrabble words hiding in the grid. The leftover letters spell a quote by Duke Ellington.

ABLED	DUMBO	RAKUS
AMPED	EXING	RUBEL
ARAME	FEDEX	RUBUS
ARENE	FESTS	SAYED
BANDA	GATER	SIDHE
BARCA	GORMS	SIGLA
BIGGY	HIJRA	SKORT
BINER	HIREE	SMUSH
BOHOS	HONGI	SNARF
BROTH	HOSEY	SOCAS
BRUNG	KOJIS	TELCO
CALOS	KORAS	TENDU
CHAIS	KVELL	TENGE
COLBY	LILTS	TIKKA
CRITS	LOUMA	TOEAS
CUVEE	NEDDY	UMAMI
DEMIC	ODAHS	URSID
DIFFS	PERPS	YUPPY
DOULA	POBOY	ZOUKS
DROID	PREOP	

```
S N A R F D R O I D P T
T K Y B U E E X I N G O
I L O M L B S M U S H E
R G B R D E E T I K K A
C O O E T E D L S C A S
Y R P N D V O I L P I I
N M U I G U U L S E B J
A S F B M C L T B R V O
O F O A U A A S U P U K
S P E C C S M N I S I S
H I L D A R G U E G I K
A R A M E S A Y E D L E
D U P H O X K B A N D A
O L D H C E Y U P P Y Y
A I O N L I G N O H Y B
S B I N E A G N I Z I L
S A C E T T P J E G R O
A B R E N E R A G T B C
B I R O L A E Y E W A I
H T H O K A O L L L T H
E V O U T W P E O L S M
I S S S I H O S E Y N G
```

64. 6-LETTER SCRABBLE WORDS

Find all the Scrabble words hiding in the grid.
The leftover letters spell a quote by Fran Lebowitz.

ADZING	LOONIE
APORIA	LUBING
ARENES	MATIER
ARIARY	MENUDO
CABLER	MIRINS
CARDIO	MUGHAL
CENTAS	OSETRA
CHUPPA	PITTAS
CYCLIN	POSTIE
ECESIC	POXIER
ENVIRO	REWORN
EOSINE	SARGOS
FLUISH	SKELLS
FRITES	STATIN
GATERS	TATSOI
HANDER	TICCED
HAZMAT	UMAMIS
LAVASH	URGING
LEPTIN	VETTER
LIGNAN	WAKAME

```
C H I L D R E T T E V R
E N A R E I T S O P E T
H E M I O O S K T D E S
L I X S R R A E T B L S
E O T E E O O L I P S A
P A P W O S F L C N A R
T I O E I N R S C R T G
I R T N T S I A E T N O
N S E T C M T N D I E S
R A A L A H E B B R C O
B L N M B S S U E E R S
A M U G H A L A C I S E
T H E S I Y C E V T H T
A R E R N L S N B A O R
T L O O N I E H N M L A
E P T A C A R D I O S Y
A O A F Y S E I T E U O
P D M L C R T B M R E A
P U Z U L E A A G T A N
U N A I I T K I T D F U
H E H S N A N N R I T O
C M C H W G H E A A N T
```

65. I'M NUMBER ONE: 2010s

Find all the recording artists hiding in the grid.
The leftover letters spell a quote by Eminem.

ADELE

BAAUER

[THE] BLACK EYED
   PEAS

BRUNO MARS

EMINEM

FAR EAST
   MOVEMENT

FLO RIDA

FUN.

GOTYE

JOHN LEGEND

KATY PERRY

KELLY CLARKSON

KESHA

LADY GAGA

LORDE

MACKLEMORE

MILEY CYRUS

PHARRELL WILLIAMS

PINK

RIHANNA

ROBIN THICKE

RYAN LEWIS

TAIO CRUZ

TAYLOR SWIFT

USHER

```
T N R T A G A G Y D A L
J O H N L E G E N D U O
S S T E I S H A I R D R
T K O M L C O R M E E D
B R Y E T E O P H U K E
E A A V G L D H A S C M
R L T O F B S A U R I I
O C T M W L B R H A H N
M Y Y T T A Y R M M T E
E L Y S A C C E I O N M
L L R A Y K C L L N I E
K E I E L E S L S U B M
C K L R O Y K W A R O L
A I L A R E A I A B R N
M D T F S D T L F I Y G
H T I H W P Y L M U A K
I N A D I E P I O F N F
U N U N F A E A N Y L A
B O K S T S R M U T E M
A N N A H I R S A K W I
N G N E W E Y F R I I E
N T A I O C R U Z D S S
```

66. WE ARE STAR STUFF

Find all the constellations hiding in the grid.
The leftover letters spell a quote and its speaker.

AQUARIUS

AQUILA

ARIES

BOÖTES

CANIS MAJOR

CANIS MINOR

CAPRICORNUS

CASSIOPEIA

CENTAURUS

CYGNUS

ERIDANUS

FORNAX

GEMINI

GRUS

HYDRA

LIBRA

LYNX

LYRA

MENSA

NORMA

OPHIUCHUS

ORION

PAVO

PEGASUS

PISCES

SAGITTARIUS

SCORPIUS

URSA MAJOR

URSA MINOR

VELA

VIRGO

VOLANS

VULPECULA

```
U K M V U L P E C U L A
R S E T O O B S E E S P
S L N Y G G O U U U R E
A S S Y R R E S N S C O
M C A Q U I L A N T A H
A O Q G S V D G R E P S
J R U O I I T E A B R R
O P A S R T S P B U I T
R I R E E I T C R C C L
E U I I M C O A A E O Y
M S U R P B S N R A R N
C E S A N R I I T I N X
E O V O K S E S P E U E
N O R P M U S M Y P S S
T M O A U N R I F O U E
A E J T A G O N N I H T
U O F L H Y E O G S C G
R R O Y O C U R E S U N
U V R R D T H E M A I O
S D N A O R E R I C H O
O S A R D Y H E N V P E
L T X U R S A M I N O R
```

Answer on page 186.

67. "STAR WARS"

Find all the answers from the "Star Wars" franchise hiding in the grid. The leftover letters spell a quote spoken by Obi-Wan Kenobi.

ADMIRAL ACKBAR

ALDERAAN

CHEWBACCA

CLOUD CITY

COUNT DOOKU

DARTH MAUL

DEATH STAR

ENDOR

FELUCIA

GAMORREAN

GEONOSIS

GREEDO

HAN SOLO

HOTH

JABBA THE HUTT

JAWA

LANDO

LEIA

LUKE

MACE WINDU

MOS EISLEY
    CANTINA

NABOO

OBI-WAN

OTOH GUNGA

PADMÉ AMIDALA

SABÉ

TATOOINE

UTAPAU

WICKET

YAVIN

YODA

```
N T H M A C E W I N D U
A E R F O L R C E I S O
E W H O A T D G I O V T
R E S A D J E E D D O O
R I H I S N F E R P D H
O O W A E R E I T A N G
M S A N N R L E C N A U
A E R I G G U Y L F L N
G C I T E A C L O D U G
C R C N P O I E U A A A
T T E A B A D D U M D
T T T C B I B Y C K H M
A U E Y J W E A I O T I
T H K E L A E L T O R R
O E C L S N W H Y D A A
O H I S I L O A C T D L
I T W I S L V A S N L A
N A L E O I O H D U I C
E B A S N V T O K O I K
N B N O O A G E B C Y B
P A D M E A M I D A L A
H J T D G H I N G S N R
```

68. PRESIDENTIAL MEDAL OF FREEDOM IN THE ARTS

Find all the medal winners hiding in the grid. The leftover letters spell a quote by Georgia O'Keeffe.

ADAMS	FRANKLIN	PRICE
BAILEY	FULLER	RAYE
BALANCHINE	GOLDWYN	RIVERA
BALL	GRAHAM	ROCKWELL
BASIE	HAYES	RUBENSTEIN
BERLIN	HEPBURN	SILLS
BLAKE	HESTON	SINATRA
COPLAND	HOPE	STERN
DOMINGO	JOHNS	WAYNE
DOUGLAS	KAYE	WELTY
DYLAN	L'AMOUR	WHITE
ELIOT	LYNN	WIESEL
ELLINGTON	MORENO	WILDER
FITZGERALD	PECK	WILSON
FORD	POITIER	WYETH

```
T O D L A R E G Z T I F
C B N O L R L Y N N R O
R E A E U E E A A A L R
T R L L E G W V N R A D
O L P P A H L K I N M E
M I O S O N L A C R O E
A N C P G I C L S O U C
H O E O N W T H L N R I
A T W H I T E I I A U R
R S W F M B O R E N B P
G E L U O L L N D R E S
O H I L D N Y A E C N M
L Y E L I A B D K H S A
D A N E W S L A O E T D
W Y O R F I Y J L I E A
Y T L E W E M I T S I R
N H W I L S O N S A N T
E A I R T T R T S B T A
H T E Y W H E P B U R N
A K S E S R N A L Y D I
C O E U N R O H A Y E S
A E L L I N G T O N G E
```

Answer on page 186.

69. DICKENS CHARACTERS

Find all the Dickensian names hiding in the grid. The leftover letters spell a quote from "Nicholas Nickleby."

ADAMS
[THE] ARTFUL DODGER
BARKIS
BAZZARD
BELLE
BETSY
BIDDY
BITZER
CHARLEY BATES
DAVID COPPERFIELD
DR. PAYNE
DUFF
DURDLES
FAGIN
FRED
GRAINGER
HUGH

KENGE
KROOK
LILIAN
LITTIMER
LOWTEN
MR. BROWNLOW
MR. FEZZIWIG
NANCY
NICHOLAS NICKLEBY
NODDY BOFFIN
OLIVER TWIST
SCROOGE
SMIKE
STAGG
SYDNEY CARTON
TINY TIM
TOOTS
TRABB

```
T H E P F L D F C A I L
Y N K O O R K F H O G I
C F P W A S E U A A I L
N R T Z I K T D R G W I
A E Z K I B A I L N I A
N A R M E M R D E G Z N
B A S L S I T L Y G Z I
B S L T Y Y F E B R E C
A E O N D O U I A A F H
R O T D N T L F T I R O
T E I S E H D R E N M L
T B N I Y N O E S G R A
I S G Y C T D P O E B S
N T I T A U G P H R R N
Y A E W R P E O S E O I
T G J D T O R C R M W C
I G L K O R R D E I N K
M E Y E N O E I Z T L L
S O F N O M E V T T O E
E T H G U H I A I I W B
N G E E A G A D B L I Y
N N I F F O B Y D D O N
```

Answer on page 187.

70. BATMAN TV SOUND EFFECTS

Find all the sound effects hiding in the grid.
The leftover letters spell a quote spoken by Batman.

AIEEE	KLONK	THWAPE
AIIEEE	KRUNCH	THWAPP
BAM	OOOOFF	UGGH
BANG	OUCH	URKK
BAP	OWWW	VRONK
BIFF	PAM	WHACK
BLOOP	PLOP	WHAMM
BLURP	POW	WHAP
BOFF	QUNCKKK	ZAM
BONK	RAKKK	ZAP
CLANK	RIP	ZGRUPPP
CLUNK	SLOSH	ZLONK
CRASH	SOCK	ZLOPP
CRR-AAACK	SPLA-A-T	ZLOTT
CRRAACK	SPLOOSH	ZOK
CRUNCH	SWA-A-P	ZOWIE
EEE-YOW	SWISH	ZZZZZWAP
GLIPP	THUNK	
KAYO	THWACK	

```
K L E A I I E E E H W O
L T S G O E R Q I C H O
O O B I E N U W W N A O
N Y R I K N G E O U C O
K N A L C N V E Z R K F
T S K K A E T M P C K F
T A K B A B N P A O R F
O K K S A T P A W P U I
L O O M R U R P O O L B
Z C A U R R P A Y S H L
K Z E G C O R H E P Y U
S N Z B L H O W E L U R
T L O Z H S Z P E A O P
N F O R Z I A W H A M M
F T B S V W P S H T K E
R O A O H S A D S N T O
A B R T N R I P O W W W
T H W A C K L L P A B I
G H T L N O Z O A I E H
R T U U O O M P A O L G
R N H S R P P A W H T G
K T H C N U R K S O W U
```

71. SONDHEIM SONGS

Find all the Stephen Sondheim songs hiding in the grid. The leftover letters spell a quote by Sondheim.

AGONY

AH, MISS

AH, PARIS!

ANOTHER HUNDRED PEOPLE

ANY MOMENT

BARCELONA

BEING ALIVE

[SEND IN THE] CLOWNS

COMEDY TONIGHT

EPIPHANY

GOD, THAT'S GOOD!

[I'M STILL] HERE

I READ

JOHANNA

LIAISONS

LIKE IT WAS

LOVELY

LOVING YOU

[GETTING] MARRIED [TODAY]

MORE

NO LIFE

NOW YOU KNOW

OUR TIME

POOR BABY

POOR THING

PRETTY LADY

REMEMBER?

SIMPLE

SUNDAY

[THERE WON'T BE] TRUMPETS

WAIT

[ANYONE CAN] WHISTLE

YOUR FAULT

```
S A W T I E K I L A R P
T L U A F R U O Y T I R
E E N Y N A H P I P E E
P L O V I N G Y O U W T
M P O O R B A B Y I H T
U O T V S D E H L F I Y
R E B M E M E R O A S L
T P I S A L N I W J T A
N D A E R I Y A R T L D
E E T A H M I S S R E Y
M R H N E D T N E L A E
O D G O V O W M P D S M
M N I L I O P M N N I I
Y U N E L G I U O G R T
N H O C A S S S L N A R
A R T R G T I T I I P U
T E Y A N A O M F H H O
B H D B I H R O E T A A
I T E L E T N R G R G O
R O M D B D E E E O R O
U N O W Y O U K N O W T
O A C F C G H Y A P O S
```

72. "GAME OF THRONES"

Find all the "Game of Thrones" words and phrases hiding in the grid. The leftover letters spell a quote spoken by Cersei.

AEMON	MARGAERY
ARYA	MYCAH
BENJEN	PETYR
BRAAVOS	PYCELLE
BRAN	RENLY
BRONN	RICKON
CATELYN	ROBB
DAENERYS	ROBERT BARATHEON
DIREWOLF	SAMWELL TARLY
EDDARD STARK	SANDOR
EDMURE	SANSA
HOSTER TULLY	STANNIS
JAIME	THE WALL
JEOR	TYRION
JOFFREY	TYWIN
JON ARRYN	VARYS
KHAL DROGO	WIGHTS
MACE	WINTERFELL

```
S A M W E L L T A R L Y
A E W I D D H E N Y O L
N M U N D P M L A Y T L
S O H T A E M U M G A U
A N R E R R M Y R A R T
B B O R D E B O C E C R
R E B F S R O D N A S E
O N E E T F T L T R H T
N J R L A H Y E R Y O S
N E T L R N L R K A O O
Y N B E K Y Y E H V S H
R Y A C N T O U A S E W
R M R Y E I T A L T M N
A F A P O R R Y D H I Y
N L T R O B S U R G A D
O O H Y G I Y E O I J S
J W E T W A R H G W O I
E E O E R I E E O I F N
O R N S N O N R M I F N
R I C K O N E D Y D R A
L D T H E W A L L E E T
G R O U N D D V A R Y S
```

73. SERIF FONTS

Find all the fonts hiding in the grid. The
leftover letters spell a quote and its speaker.

ALDUS

ALEXANDRIA

ALGERIAN

ANTIQUA

ARNO

ASTER

AURORA

BASKERVILLE

BEMBO

BODONI

BOOKMAN

BULMER

CARTIER

CASLON

CATULL

COCHIN

DIDOT

EMERSON

EXCELSIOR

FAIRFIELD

FOOTLIGHT

GOUDY

JANSON

JOANNA

KORINNA

MELIOR

MEMPHIS

MILLER

MINION

PERPETUA

RENAULT

REQUIEM

SISTINA

TRAJAN

UTOPIA

```
I D E M E R S O N O N O
A T A I P O T U T T H I
U L N L K M R E M L U B
Q U O L F A E T Y P E N
I A A E U N I M S S O O
T N M R O E T T P L H B
N E O I I A R N S H E G
A R N D T L A A H M I A
A I E T L G C S B T H S
M O R Q U E L O R D B E
P R E D U R I A C A D A
E B L E N I J F I H E T
R E T S A A E S R X I H
P O U L N N X M C I D N
E E L L I V R E K S A B
T B C A T U L L L M E F
U B E A S S U I K A J J
A T H G I L T O O F A O
T I F O S K O R I N N A
U L R U E B D D B R S N
E B O D O N I N A G O N
U I A Y S U D L A T N A
```

74. SANS-SERIF FONTS

Find all the fonts hiding in the grid. The leftover letters spell a quote and its speaker.

ARIAL	HELVETICA
AVENIR	HOBO
BAUHAUS	IMPACT
BETECKNA	INDUSTRIA
CABIN	KABEL
CALIBRI	LATO
CASEY	MEIRYO
COMPACTA	MICROGRAMMA
CORBEL	MYRIAD
DOTUM	OPTIMA
ECOFONT	ROBOTO
ERAS	SYNTAX
EUROCRAT	TAHOMA
EUROSTILE	TIRESIAS
FRUTIGER	UBUNTU
FUTURA	UNIVERS
GOTHAM	VERDANA

```
E  T  T  O  T  I  Y  P  O  G  F  A
R  R  C  A  B  I  R  D  O  T  U  M
A  P  A  H  C  O  R  B  E  L  T  O
T  Y  P  S  Y  I  H  E  I  S  U  H
C  T  M  R  H  E  C  R  S  L  R  A
A  A  I  N  D  U  S  T  R  I  A  T
P  E  U  R  O  S  T  I  L  E  A  C
M  I  C  R  O  G  R  A  M  M  A  S
O  A  F  O  T  B  U  E  I  O  F  E
C  N  H  N  F  D  O  T  V  O  W  I
N  A  G  T  H  O  P  T  N  I  U  M
A  D  V  A  O  O  N  I  O  U  N  N
Y  R  L  E  A  G  B  T  N  T  B  U
G  E  I  U  N  A  A  T  G  E  A  U
A  V  S  A  C  I  A  M  W  I  C  L
N  T  H  A  L  R  R  Y  A  D  I  U
K  R  A  B  C  E  L  R  E  V  T  I
C  S  U  O  A  L  B  I  F  O  E  R
E  M  R  S  Y  N  T  A  X  R  V  O
T  U  B  E  R  T  B  D  K  R  L  I
E  N  G  H  F  R  U  T  I  G  E  R
B  A  U  H  A  U  S  U  R  S  H  T
```

Answer on page 188.

75. DON'T PANIC

Find all the "Hitchhiker's Guide to the Galaxy" characters hiding in the grid. The leftover letters spell a quote from the guide.

AGRAJAG

ANJIE

[THE GREAT GREEN] ARKLESEIZURE

BENJY

COLIN

DEEP THOUGHT

[ARTHUR] DENT

EDDIE

EFFRAFAX [OF WUG]

ELVIS [PRESLEY]

ENID [KAPELSEN]

FENCHURCH

FOOK

FORD [PREFECT]

FRANKIE

GAIL [ANDREWS]

GARGRAVARR

GARKBIT

GOOGLEPLEX [STARTHINKER]

HACTAR

[GAG] HALFRUNT

JUDICIARY PAG

LALLAFA

LUNKWILL

MARVIN

PRAK

[QUESTULAR] RONTOK

ROOSTA

SLARTIBARTFAST

THOR

TRILLIAN

VEET [VOOJAGIG]

WONKO [THE SANE]

ZAPHOD [BEEBLEBROX]

ZARQUON

```
J U D I C I A R Y P A G
A F E E T O F W C E R A
L E E I N I A S O A K R
B N P J K T L N L S L G
T C T N O N L I I U E R
T H H A Z T A V N H S A
E U O D A G L R T E E V
M R U R P E U A F N I A
T C G O H W N M I O Z R
S H H F O O K D S T U R
A G T N D M W A S S R O
F O K E D D I E I O E O
T O V E L P L Y N F U S
R G S E F R L T F U L T
A L A T H A O R I N G A
B E N J Y K A I A N Z R
I P I N A F T L E R A S
T L T E A R L L L T R A
R E R X H I G I C T Q C
A X T I B K R A G H U H
L I K E R C H N A N O H
S A V E H A L F R U N T
```

76. TALK LIKE AN EGYPTIAN

Find all the mythological figures hiding in the grid.
The leftover letters spell a quote and its speaker.

AKEN	MEHIT
AKER	MENHIT
AMMIT	MERETSEGER
AMUN	MESKHENET
ANHUR	MIN
ANUBIS	MNEVIS
ANUKET	NEITH
APEP	NEKHBET
APIS	OSIRIS
ATUM	PTAH
BASTET	QEBUI
BAT	RENENUTET
BUCHIS	SATET
GEB	SEKER
HAPI	SEKHMET
HATHOR	SHU
HEQET	SOBEK
ISIS	TAWERET
IUSAASET	THOTH
KHNUM	WADJET
KHONSU	WADJ-WER
MAAT	WOSRET

```
W H A H A T P T I M D E
A L S I U E N T G W I T
M H I H I S S A S O V A
N A S S S A M W T T N A
E T I M M A U E N U E D
V E B I M S T R K G K R
I J U U E U A E A T H T
S D N B N I T T T H B A
E A A E T I N T M T E C
K W N Q H E Q E T A T N
E E T B K E S R C A L K
R E K A K K L S E D H H
E T H E H E W O T N R O
G E B E T A U W U T H N
E O N A D T E M H K E S
S E B J S I T S E A B U
T I W U O T H O T H H S
E E P T C R E H V A I E
R T A A U H A T T R H T
E A P H E P I H I I T R
M E N H I T O S U T E H
P A S U N R O R A M I N
```

77. POLISH CITIES

Find all the cities hiding in the grid. The leftover letters spell a quote and its speaker.

BYTOM

CHORZÓW

CZĐSTOCHOWA

ELBLĐG

GDAĐSK

GDYNIA

GLIWICE

KALISZ

KATOWICE

KIELCE

KOSZALIN

KRAKÓW

LEGNICA

ŁÓDĐ

LUBLIN

OLSZTYN

OPOLE

PŁOCK

POZNAĐ

RADOM

RZESZÓW

SOSNOWIEC

SZCZECIN

TARNÓW

TORUĐ

TYCHY

WAŁBRZYCH

WARSZAWA

WŁOCŁAWEK

WROCŁAW

ZABRZE

```
M O S G T P E O L P L E
A S K D F O R H U A P P
I N E Y K L Z A B R Z E
S S O N N A E C L O N C
N E C I W I L G I D I I
I K R A K O W I N T I W
L O N H A E Z K S I P O
A W O H C O T S E Z C T
Z P A L I T N N E E H A
S S E L O D Z A N Z O K
O I S R B C A D I K R N
K O U A N R P G C L Z Y
E N B D A O Z O E E O F
W E L O T W L Y Z I W F
A Y O M W P A S C N U D
L O N M R T S Z Z H A E
C E I W O N S O S T T N
O L A P C T N Y A R Y C
L B O O L N Y R D H A N
W L I T A I N B C O N W
E A A R W O T Y H U R R
U G B I W N T S T E I N
```

78. RULERS OF JAPAN

Find all the emperors and empresses hiding in the grid. The leftover letters spell a quote and its speaker.

ANKAN	KEITAI	RICHU
ANKO	KENZO	SAGA
ANNEI	KINMEI	SEIWA
BIDATSU	KOAN	SENKA
BURETSU	KOBUN	SHIRAKAWA
GENMEI	KOGEN	SHOMU
HEIZEI	KOGYOKU	SUININ
HORIKAWA	KOKEN	SUIZEI
INGYO	KONIN	SUJIN
JIMMU	KONOE	SUSHUN
JINGU	MURAKAMI	SUZAKU
JITO	NINKEN	TENMU
JUNNA	NINMYO	TOBA
JUNNIN	NINTOKU	UDA
KANMU	OJIN	YOMEI
KAZAN	REIZEI	

```
M U Y G G R O A N O D F
A M T H E Z E R W Y A U
N N S A N A Z A K M M D
E E S E M S C E I N N N
D T K U E A N T A I I O
F T K N I H E K T N J E
A A O M I Z O I I P U E
R W N A N N E I E O S R
A A I N O Z N I K J U D
O K N E I W K U Y I Z E
Y A S E S W S O J M A J
G R H E R T M A B M K I
N I O E E E O B V U U N
I H M R I E K O S K N G
E S U S H U N T O R Y U
M B R N O W A Y E A K U
N L A N R D G T H O K H
I O K N I O O Y T O O C
K Y A B K N J N K T G I
O A M K A A I E Z I E R
O D I O W N N U N J N O
J U N N A K N E S A G A
```

79. IT TAKES TWO

Find both halves of the famous pairs hiding in the grid, only half of which has been provided. The leftover letters spell a Shakespeare quote. A complete word list is on page 190.

ABBOTT & _____

ANTONY & _____

BERT & _____

BOGART & _____

BONNIE & _____

CAPTAIN & _____

CHEECH & _____

FRED & _____

HALL & _____

HANSEL & _____

JACK & _____

LAUREL & _____

LAVERNE & _____

LEWIS & _____

PENN & _____

ROCKY & _____

ROMEO & _____

SIMON & _____

SONNY & _____

THELMA & _____

```
G H A R D Y O O D N G I
G C A C S H Y N O T N A
T E G N L O O O E T O M
D E N I S A N N G O H L
H H T P A E R N R B C E
T C L Y D E L K Y B I H
N G O I V A S E T A O T
S S L A U U L N N E P C
H S L R R R W I E E E T
S O E R I E A Y R L O W
T L T H H T H K A L T J
I E S S P J A C K I H U
A K O A I L L O L N S L
A N C L S Y L R G N O I
B U L L W I N K L E O E
E F E D N B M I L T I T
R R O G O E M O R N G E
T A P G H S U T N R I L
T G A I L I L O E I N L
T R T B S W B T E M G E
T F R E D E E R N I E R
O B A C A L L R R O R W
```

80. WORD SANDWICHES

Find all the words missing their first and last letters hiding in the grid. The list is presented alphabetically (once the letters have been restored), and none of the answers will end with the letter S. The leftover letters spell a quote and its speaker. A complete word list is on page 191.

__BAT__	__HOSE__	__AXES__
__BOAR__	__LIMA__	__EGG__
__CUT__	__RANK__	__ILK__
__DIE__	__DUCAT__	__IRK__
__GIN__	__MOT__	__OLD__
__PAR__	__LOWER__	__RATIO__
__PRO__	__LOB__	__LEAS__
__WAS__	__REED__	__REST__
__WHIR__	__YEN__	__HEM__
__ALEE__	__VIE__	__HORN__
__URN__	__NOW__	__ELS__
__ACT__	__ACROSS__	__ESTER__
__HANG__	__AMEN__	__IDES__
__HID__	__ATTIC__	__INDIES__

```
I C M N O T N A S A H N
D W H I C Y H E S T S O
R E K A D I E U E T A H
A T N L N O N L Y L W S
E L O L S G G N I G A T
U M W E S T E R N R N B
B K N E Y S T S E O A P
N U D W O I A C R E R H
E S R H I R B P S E D E
L L C N A A A L S E O Y
T C A C T I B T B O F D
I F F L H E O O I R W M
E I V I E D L N A O I T
T H I M M G T H O R N Y
T N G A E S G S K L D A
S F D X E Y E Y K L I M
E L G D L A T T I C E W
X O I A L A C R O S S E
A W H I R L M H A M T L
L E D U C A T E I P E S
C R A N K Y L G N D A H
H Y E N A P A C U T E A
```

Answers

1. STATE OF THE ART

A good painting to me has always been like a friend. It keeps me company, comforts, and inspires.

2. TONGUE-TIED

England and America are two countries separated by the same language.

3. "THE HUNGER GAMES"

Only I keep wishing I could think of a way to … to show the Capitol they don't own me.

4. OLD TESTAMENT

A thorough knowledge of the Bible is worth more than a college education.

5. ASTRONAUTS A-C

```
M Y S Y E V O O B T N E
A R L Y C K L U L R A E
L B L A B I C L O A M T
W A U O F H B B O E R S
A K B F L W L E M O O K
H E O I Y N A R F D B E
C R W R D D H T I A N C
D U E D A C A S E W A Y
O B R M R A S O L L R E
N R S B B R A N D R M R
C O O P E R B E A N S A
N W X K D A I B L B T C
A N A E G R M B L S R R
M R I I O S U U E T O I
P H A E C R F G N B N P
A N A S S O D A I S G P
H S O C R I N F M A E E
C N H D R R A R S V D N
H O E B E S M I A R E T
I O A C Y U T E N D D E
A R S T C O L L I N S T
O A N D S C A L D R I N
```

Mystery creates wonder, and wonder is the basis of man's desire to understand.

6. LIVE MÁS

```
E V A M A C I J E S R Y
Q S O E N C H I L A D A
U L Q U E S A D I L L A
E H C E L E D E C L U D
S O H C A N I N H I S A
O T I R R U B T I T A N
R Z A G L E A A L R T A
E L I C A S R M E O I P
H T U R O N R A R T N M
C O D P O Z O L E A R E
N S E R O H Z E L M A A
A T U A L F C F L T C C
R A G R O H O C E E R A
S D T Y U S N T N O R R
O A E R E G P S O V E N
V D R R O Y O T H E I E
E O U N G T L R I H S A
U C A N I L L L D C E S
H D L U E U O P I I T A
A I Q N M M E X I V T D
C A O F R I J O L E S A
T O L L A G E D O C I P
```

Every single laundromat, grocery store, everything is called Lupita in Mexico.

7. GEMSTONES

```
I T A D D O A E R E W E
L A P O I A G Z D R L S
E N I R A M A U Q A B A
N Z I N M P T G P L J P
O A G E O M E I O E S P
T N B T N U S O Z X T H
S I C N D L D T Y A O I
N T T I A S R B B N E R
O E K Z T A U C E D A E
O U U O U R S E E R T N
M L N Q R D I T A I Y I
I E Z H Q O I N M T E L
Y A I R U N E M E E I A
N E T Y O Y O U T T C M
A N E S I X E I H I T R
P O S P S M R S Y L S U
E E S S E U R N S O A O
H D I R Z A O A T D N T
C E A A E C R Y O O U C
A L N O R B N L L H Y A
D E T I T A M E H R D M
I R Z T E N R A G E I T
```

I adore wearing gems, but not because they are mine. You can't possess radiance, you can only admire it.

8. GREEK GODS

```
H E M E R A T H E N A
E Z T A R T A R U S T
R E H I E B X A T T L
M U E F D Y E I E S L
E S U T N O P R I U D
S O N P Y H R M O T I
S U S A S C E H C S E
N U S E S T H O P E F
C O N Y R O S E R A N
S T A A N N N E T H C
H A O S R O B O T P H
E W N I N U I G R E T
N E O R S S E D A H W
I L D L I B E T A E C
H E I T O N E N W R A
H O E A C O A N T A R
O M S I L T S T E P H
A T O T O C H T A O O
S N P S A P H O L L E
R E T E M E D O N L B
O N A H R P A R T O E
```

The battlefield is a scene of constant chaos. The winner will be the one who controls that chaos. —Napoleon Bonaparte

9. ROMAN GODS

```
W H E N F E R O N I A A
R C H L A C E O L O G I
S T O S O D R L I S C O
M R V N E R A E T H T E
A V S M I R S S B I E N
R U E G E A R M S I L O
S I T S I D G A N U L F
U U V E T E R M I N U S
N O N U J A E N C U S S
M D B I P E T S E L A P
U M E O R P I I R L O T
T H L E O I P Y E W E I
R L L M S L U S S N L F
O A O I E N J Q U D S H
V N N E R W A T C N S W
A U A A P E P A R L A R
U T L I I E N G O U V J
R R B C N D I P U C R O
O O X S A T U R N I E I
R F N G G N L O V N N E
A S J O H N B A R A I R
Y M O R Y R U C R E M E
```

When archaeologists discover the missing arms of Venus de Milo, they will find she was wearing boxing gloves. —John Barrymore

10. WINNING SPELLING WORDS

```
C O L U X U R I A N C E
A M P E H C R A M E D N
S C H A P P E A R N Y I
C A M B I S T U N A M F
E H E I S W T I T H S E
T O L F R A C A S L I R
I U T O L U C L E A S R
C A R U R P P R R C O E
I O C N N O O L L A H S
S A U N R S P C I I T C
M M I L I E U H R G N I
U A A C T M M H Y E A N
E I N R Y O U I N L X O
C I N N A M E Z C E L M
Y O O E O G R N S L P E
L U O R N K D O E L U A
E E T T E N G I V L I D
D S A N G A A S N G W U
I O R N U C T R L E A E
A S T D L K A O B V I D
N O D R E U G T R I U S
K E N K D R A L U O P O
```

Company names without clear pronunciation or spelling won't last. —David Rusenko

11. SCI-FI NOVELS

```
J U R A S S I C P A R K
A R E N D E Z V O U S X
R E E Y O L U T E N L E
L I M T A P N G D M G N
E Y A N T S R L O B U O
P B G E U A I E I A L C
O I S R T W M R Y T A I
S T R D E A I M A T E D
I M E L M R T D G L D E
T A D I I O C L E E O S
R I N H T F A R M F C P
O H E C N T T O O I N H
N I N O I H N W A E O E
I E V O E E O W M L S R
C A U T L W C E P D A E
O F A D K O D N E E E E
L O E R N R E E D A R A
N E B S I L A V U R T A
N C K P R D T A N T H O
T H E I W S F R E H G U
T V E N U S U B I K I U
R E Y A W E T A G U L F
```

Are you telling me you built a time machine out of a DeLorean? —"Back to the Future"

12. PLANT GENERA

```
S J S E I X O R A U A S
O T M U I L L A E R I A
L L H C L I V R I P S N
A I C A C A I N O C 4 M
N G I L B C G M S N D P
U N N Y A E O A D O R T
M E O P N E N I R O A U
U G C T A H G A O T I N
I E Y U O O M U R S S T
G H P S F R X A V I S A
Y E E E A A C A S U A I
Z M R N S L I A L H C M
Y A U I N E V N R I F O
S N S I R E E I E E S R
U T D O B M A N A G X E
C H D A L O I T T L U P
R U E A I B R O H P U B
E R F L S O W D E R N P
U I A E R U A T N E C H
Q U A N S C C H L E R I
S M T I A N A I N D D E
O I C E N E S R F S E N
```

Just living is not enough ... One must have sunshine, freedom, and a little flower. —Hans Christian Andersen

13. POPES, PART I

The fact that I was a girl never damaged
my ambitions to be a pope or an emperor.
—Willa Cather

14. POPES, PART II

It is by God's mercy that we are saved.
May we never tire of spreading
this joyful message to the world.

15. ASTRONAUTS D-I

I don't know what you could say about a day
in which you have seen four beautiful sunsets.

16. "FAMILY GUY"

The only rock I know that stays steady,
the only institution I know that works,
is the family. —Lee Iacocca

17. ITALIAN FOOD

N O I M A L A S M A T T
E E R A T T A B A I C
T W H L E C L R O E I V
T E B E L O A E Z N O V
E E R R C A S R R E E A
I L L I S U P S O L O C
H T P C H E E R L N N A
C A F O O Z T E A O I P
C D S T I T T I L F R E
E N M T K A U S A O O L
R L I A I E C X S A C L
O I L L R C C C A T E I
E S G E P I I T G T P N
I A S A D U N I N E N I
T R G O T R E A E C I T
T A N T B O A T R N E A
E N O T A U N P P A N C
H O C O L Y C I P P N U
G B C S C A Z O R A E B
A R H I M Z E N E L P E
P A I R A V I O L I C T
S C A V A T A P P I R A

No matter where I've been overseas, the food
stinks, except in Italy. —Carmen Electra

18. FINDING MY RELIGION

Y T I N A I T S I R H C
Y T S I T N E V D A O H
U C A B U D D H I S M U
N A R E H T U L H T N R
O N O T B E L I I A E C
N A C I L G N A M F V H
D E N I W T N G S A M O
E O D U O A U M I R S F
N L I N O O S T E I I C
O S B I W I C C A A N H
M L E M H S S Y D N A R
I S P K O M O M N I I I
N M I U B D S E A S R S
A S S L L I N I M M E T
T E C I A V E A I S T S
I N O F N U Y O C I Y I
O B P U R I T S E U B T
N L A F S W A I A D S P
A M L H I V I J R N E A
L V E K A M A L S I R B
P A G A N I S M A H P N
A N D A A I R E T N A S

You cannot believe in God until you
believe in yourself. —Swami Vivekananda

19. KITCHEN AIDS

R E L E E P B M L E S S
E R R R R T R E A M E R
K S E E P R H A E M F E
C P C T A O E T O O D R
A I I T S I F T E R O O
R D L U T E B H S T E C
C E S C R F Z E A A O E
T R G T Y R G R E R B L
U U G I B S A M C A T P
N H E U L P R O A N E P
F N A C E K L M N D E A
M I P S N S I E O P I L
Y P G I D I C T P E B E
W G S B E H P E E S O I
E N L D R W R R N T V A
R I E L U M E S E L E L
C L A N I D S I R E N U
S L D L N M S T G H M T
K O L A E L D O V H I A
R R L E B E T O W E T P
O O E N U S G N O T T S
C L A D L E N N U F S S

Bless the food before us, the family
beside us, and the love between us.

20. LAKES

A G O D A L W E R L C O
M I E T O O L A Y K E W
T O R B E V N Y M G M O
N R W O O H K T Y L I E
R E E S T C A L A L C T
S R T B U C H K T R H E
A O A T L W I O M E I N
K O N E G A I V N A G O
A E R E B S T W I R A O
K N G A L T L R A I N Y
A C T H E M A E R L N A
W H R E G O O E T D A L
E A S L I V E D R O O M
A M K I N T G A A G C A
C P N D A A L C H E O L
S L T H E B C A C P M H
A A L I L L D C T I O R
B I G E E E N I N N A R
A N A E W R A T O N E B
H U R O N O G I P I N O
T V D E A C P T R W V E
A R A A G K E E O H A T

Welcome to Lake Wobegon, where all the
women are strong, all the men are good-looking,
and all the children are above average.

21. DOG BREED PLACES

I am called a dog because I fawn on those who give me anything, I yelp at those who refuse, and I set my teeth in rascals. —Diogenes

22. MOVIE MUSICALS

The greatest thing you'll ever learn is just to love and be loved in return.

23. DOWN ON THE PHARM

Walking is man's best medicine.
—Hippocrates

24. CHESS OPENINGS

I get more upset at losing at other things than chess. I always get upset when I lose at Monopoly. —Magnus Carlsen

25. ASTRONAUTS J-O

```
E D A E M N A G R O M L
A N N M A T T I N G L Y
J O N I Z U K A R N G U
O S W A L D A R N O G E
H I N Y L L E W E L L I
N M S K E L L Y W G A V
S E C N O V E R M Y E R
O J O N O W A K A C D L
N I I A A O C R N D I O
R U S G L I F E I N R V
R N O E N M R C E E B E
O M A L U W U N L L C L
T R E G A L G E E S M L
Y M R L I E S P F O L A
M C C O R N L S E N O J
E A L C N O R W O I C E
M I G O U I Y E L A K T
I L I N O L W A J R H T
C M G N U C L R S L A B
H E U O R S C E E I R R
E V A R G S U M Y K T O
L L E H C T I M U G H S
```

Language is a virus from outer space.
—William S. Burroughs

26. SPICE IT UP

```
A N D E E S E S I N A S
Y M A R J O R A M K A E
S U C L O V E S I G O S
L S U I D I E R E R W A
B T R O L R P M T L H M
C A R A W A Y S E E D E
H R Y H P H N M I I E S
I D P L T G O T L S E E
L S O C E N E L R S S E
I E W H A A I M L O L D
P E D I T S V M T H E O
O D E V U L D E U U N B
W E R E G N I G S C N E
D E E S Y P P O P A E N
E S T I W A R T A C F N
R Y D S T I L A I L O T
H R O S E M A R Y E N R
E E A R E L R T H A I
N L G S I M W A O R G T
Y E L S R A P G H F E I
G C A U H T I O N G R F
O B T R C I N N A M O N
```

Any soldier worth his salt should be antiwar.
And still there are things worth fighting for.

27. PAINT COLORS

```
E I B F R O S E S I L K
M Y L A S O P O R P E O
I U T M T C E O U L M D
L S S U J H S A Y I O T
Y X A L A G S T I N N P
T W L P C N U A O R T E
S E B R K O O N L D W A
O P D A F S M G S T I C
R A N G R K Y E E S S H
F R A U O R R R T I T J
T G S S S A R I A L A A
H L F E T L E N N V T M
R A R E U Y B E A E N U
W C E X O K P D R R I L
U I E A I S S R G M M P
L T S W U D A E E I R R
B S I E N Q R A M S E E
O Y A B R E A M O T P H
A M U N I T A L P S P T
O F M I S T Y R O S E A
F N T O P A I N T O P E
E P I R T S Y D N A C H
```

If you could say it in words
there would be no reason to paint.

28. POE STORIES

```
N A M S S E N I S U B O
O F P X O B G N O L B O
I U N S I T S O M I H A
T S D B E E D I U O N S
A I E G I L R T L N A I
N K V L D T O A U I H A
G T I A T H W C D Z O S
I E L N W H F I N I O M
S O I D G S O F E N S T
S D N S U P R I P G I S
A L T C B H E T E S L P
I O H A D I W S H K R E
E S E P L N O Y T E C C
T S B E O X P M D I B T
H O E G G E M I N L A A
R F L A E O C E A N T C
H B F R O A R C T O S L
E R R D M E K F I B W E
H E Y E B C O A P N R S
E A N N A L L E R O M L
E T A T S T A B L B H E
T H O U T T E R T H E M
```

Of puns it has been said that those
who most dislike them are those
who are least able to utter them.

29. POKÉMON

We'll coerce those creeps
into creating chaos!

30. WHAT'S COOKING?

I admire the courage and
self-reliance it takes to start your
own business and make it succeed.

31. KNOTS

When you get to the end of your
rope, tie a knot and hang on.
—Franklin Delano Roosevelt

32. SUPER BOWL MVPS

I believe that a bad Super Bowl
halftime show is still better than
a soccer game. —Ron White

33. HARRY POTTER

I Y O F L A M O C A R D
R O W E N A C T I S O U
Y D O O M E Y E D A M R
C H M O I C E O D S H A
R O C R S Y L T H R R A
P T S O I O H O W I I M
H C U O R C Y T R A B C
W H A E I N T N W A H G
E T S R U U E F N T E O
A L E Y S F D L G I L N
R Y V A B R U E I R G A
O E E F L I D U L U A G
D I R G A H L R D A S A
A R U V C M E O E R A L
H E S I K H Y N R T L L
P H S K A S O N O O A C
M A N T U I U C Y R Z I
Y N A O M A B M H H A R
N U P R I L I T E A R D
L L E B E I T A K R N O
I H V O L D E M O R T G
R O N W E A S L E Y E S

It is our choices, Harry, that show what
we truly are, far more than our abilities.

34. FRENCH FOOD

T E O U N S O U F F L E
D N T R O F E U Q O R E
R I S T A F U I N D E U
R A O P U O D R L P E Y
O R S A E I N I E O N U
H R T A S E O A D I I T
V O R E I G F L A S T A
P L E N O R T C N S A L
O E V I C A B E E O R O
E H S V I S A G P N G C
P C T U N E N N A E I O
R I O A E U O S T O R H
O U C Q D R E R V E H C
F Q I O A R F G R P E U
I L R C L N C R O H M A
T R A T A T O U I L L E
E M H T S A L Y D E I S
R L E I N E N E E R A S
O L B R T E I R B G H U
L T T R E B M E M A C O
E E L U R B E M E R C M
P O M M E D E T E R R E

To understand Europe,
you have to be a genius—or French.
—Madeleine Albright

35. ASTRONAUTS P-S

Y O T R A W E T S S U K
N D E O W B E I H P K N
N R S G Y D D A E R I A
A O I S T E R S P I N V
T F R P C R I A A N S I
L F A O I H T T R G E L
I A P H S R M E D I R L
N T C A I T I A E S U
L S Y C R S M T H W S
A Y K W M K S X R T T P
R H S A E H E I E T Y I
O E N H A D V R G O L L
M L A S N E T H I C L L
I W L I R I E S W S I I
N T O B O C C A S U E H
G P P K T R U O C E R P
E E B O C S F E U G O P
R I C H A R D S S I A N
O E S S A I U N S I T H
S E R E I G H T L E R W
S O S N O D D E S R G L
R E H C T A S O O R D A

You know, being a test pilot isn't always
the healthiest business in the world.

36. MOONS

C A L L I R R H O E A T
H M E T I S E E K U U R
E A D E A R T I S R T H
E L A I S R D S O Y O A
D T N E G I C O M D N D
E H C H X S C H I O O R
M E G A C L I T E M E A
Y A R R L A N R D E D S
N P N P O L O O E T N T
A E B A E K I S O N O E
G L K L I L O S A N P A
P A P Y G T H I T D S H
A R H K L S N A H O H P
S A O E I A Y E E D E I
I E B N L G K U B M R S
T N O T E I R H E E M A
H P S T S O K N R U I P
E N E C P C M E I T P H
E K N A N A E M N M P O
O N A R N S D R O T E H
E T R P U T T A M H B U
T H Y O N E D C E D H A

Three things cannot be long hidden:
the sun, the moon, and the truth.
—Buddha

37. OPI LOVE U

```
L U T R A E H T E E W S
C K E P A S S I O N C O
N S E M I S T F D S L A
R G B I E L U Y N C O F
V H I R A C B N A U G E
E I M H H N A E L T G S
S O A S X G S N R E B A
P Y I N N Y T O E L M C
E A M U I U I D Z I I Y
R R R J J F L I T T D N
O P N A G O L S I T N A
S R E C G R E O L L I F
Y A A N A I M L G E G F
F L P N S U Y I N V H I
U I T P G I H T L I T T
T S R B H E E A T X H I
U E L S N I A I G E S S
R U A T T A R R R N T T
E Q E O G D T E O Y O U
R C T A L T A R E G O W
A A Y A A R O T N A L L
S J T Y B A B Y E H O N
```

Luck consists largely of hanging on by your fingernails until things start to go your way. —Aaron Allston

38. AUTOBOTS

```
F B U M P E R E W I N D
R E B M O C H C A E B O
R S U N S T R E A K E R
E E D O A M P J I S B T
R O T P E C R E P T R O
J G R I M L O C K A A H
P A C B U H W T I H W R
W L Z E T H L L S R N A
I S I Z I R B R G I H T
N T O R L R A N S I O C
D E L F E E S C N A S H
C L E A G M W F K L T E
H L K R I S E E C S E T
A E I R C R R N A K E T
R I A F N S V E B I L B
G G N O F K E L T D J L
E R N I T J U K U S A A
R A B E P R U P O O W S
I P N G R S S M U M O T
P P T I S E P I P N S E
M L U S P R I O M E C R
R E D A L E R T T E R H
```

Freedom is the right of all sentient beings. —Optimus Prime

39. DECEPTICONS

```
Y O U S E G A R R A B T
T R E T S A M R O T O M
I O L T H G U A L S N O
L L L W I L D R I D E R
K A E B R E S A L T C F
C K W A L C R O Z A R I
A S G H H A T F D B U O
S M A E R C S R A T S S
N O R A T A A T H A H W
A V E D E G V X O R E I
R E W S S T E A A F R N
R R G T O T I P G U F D
E K R R R U N B C E E L
P I E O U E N K R A E E
P L V N L O U D D E A B
A L O G A S C E W R V M
R K T N H T N S U A A O
C T I S G D C M W H V B
S Y K O O H B O Y O E E
U L O S E L A M E G N V
A T R O E C N U O P O I
N B O M B S H E L L M D
```

You still fight for the weak. That is why you lose! —Megatron

40. DEWEY DECIMAL SYSTEM

```
F R E N C H H K E U S M
A I Y G O L O C E Y A N
B V S P R I N T S E E H
A V E H S A T T G I R O
N R M S R F E C N L O G
O W A U C M S T I U R F
I L S I S S T Y S F F R
G N G P O I G M S L T H
I O A H M O C S E R Y A
L C E E L E E G C G M M
E G N A H C E A O A I Y
R T N T T N S L R N H S
O A H S D M O D P P U R
C E R I A H A S A D Y S
H E S E C R I R T N R C
E I R Y B S G E A M O I
T D S E I O M T D O N S
E P G T I Z O O L O G Y
A L N L O B D K T K N H
A O B W A R T S S S L P
M I N I N G Y E D G U E
B P L A B T O R O L O C
```

Human behavior flows from three main sources: desire, emotion, and knowledge. —Plato

41. "THE SIMPSONS"

I used to be with it, but then they changed
what "it" was, and now what I'm with isn't it.

42. COME RIGHT IN, SIT RIGHT DOWN

I'm plagued with indecision in
my life. I can't figure out what to
order in a restaurant. —Chuck Close

43. TALKIN' TOLKIEN

One Ring to rule them all,
One Ring to find them, One Ring to bring
them all and in the darkness bind them.

44. A BONE TO PICK

No one will ever know what "In Cold Blood"
took out of me. It scraped me right down to
the marrow of my bones. It nearly killed me.
—Truman Capote

45. ASTRONAUTS T-Z

T H A G A R D T G F O R
W H C A E V W O R D E N
H A A K M A Z T E U E V
E R L R E A S O B N L I
D A I W D N T S N U C Y
W E T H E R B E E C U O
I E M I B T G E D Z O U
S T B T H E S N N L T N
O E R E E O O R A A T G
F Y P E R T T O V W H A
F T S C N E I H E N C E
W L A R S N N T A N I T
N F O O R G H N I R L S
E H I W N O E V A E R W
T R A N M I N T O T O A
F T E A A C H E R O O R
O A S C O U N S D U E L
H O R S Z W H W O H T O
N L S D M T A E T T H A
A O T S T R I N H C I E
V N C E D W A E S F O R
B S M A L L I W O Y S

For whatever reason, I didn't succumb to
the stereotype that science wasn't for girls. ...
I never ran into a teacher or a counselor
who told me that science was for boys.

46. HORROR MOVIES

T N O I S L U P E R H E
F R E A D R E C E R T A
K R A D R A E N G N L D
A O A O I S I N N I R D
N S U N B I I L E G E I
A E S T K L T N H H A C
M M M L W E S T P T G T
R A O O N N N E O M R I
E R H O M C O S L A E O
K Y U K S E S W T R M N
C S T N A O F A E E L B
I B I O D F E J R O I G
W A E W B T R D G N N N
Y B G H I H A N E E S I
O Y N R A E T D I L E R
R T I O D L U S S M P U
C C N L E A L S T S S E
F U I L L M Y O Y T I S
U V H R V B I C W R V E
E A S H O S H R R E R O
S R E H T O R A M E E O
V I E X O R C I S T E N

There are certain rules that
one must abide by in order to
successfully survive a horror movie.

47. SPANISH 101

M Y O D R I D V O J O R
C M A R T E S I U I N P
G A A S T B A L E U B A
I D M E L A I L I Z O D
T R I I E O U I S O T R
F E O S S R N C D O S E
O M D A N A N A M C O O
B L A N C O J F M I G H
O M S E Z N C E N R A C
X O A A I T H H S E O
C O R R L H O E E E A H
V O A F U E R L D N H E
C N L C Z M O R R U B P
A A U G A C E I S L E D
L M B N R V M N E B G
I E A E A R R O Z U A T
E T I R Z G S G E B J H
N M R O I A U N R G O E
T R E S B L O I H L H H
E D R A T T L M L O L C
L Y D M A R Z O R E N E
W O R G E N P D O O D L

My driving abilities from Mexico have
helped me get through Hollywood.

48. SHAKESPEARE CHARACTERS

T H J E P O L O N I U S
E D U R T R E G F O N E
O L L D S O M T S A H R
T V I O L A O U I H U C
I N E K C U L R H P E C
I S T D Q A D E S W I O
S D U N C A N T R L U I
B F A S C F O I U I T D
F B E S E H K T T R O E
H E A S U W C U I E S L
E C T T M I I S A N N I
T E O D E S D E M O N A
O N I K N S E U O G T G
G I M W S L N S A U H O
A L U O Z N E R O L K I
B E R S T L B N E N C M
I B G R L H S I N S U E
A M L I N O R E B O P J
N Y H C F A T O G I X B
C C E A D O G B E R R Y
A G R I P P A F O I E O
O R S I N O T X E S L V

The fool doth think he is wise, but the
wise man knows himself to be a fool.

49. "DOCTOR WHO" COMPANIONS

```
D N O P Y M A N V L E V
N O I L E M A K I E R I
G N L E E L A Z C N O R
E O C O A S S V T N I N
P M C D S H I I O A D E
N M R Y A C E S R V U N
L I N W G E K L I I S S
C R O F R C V O A L C O
U C R S A I E R W L Y O
H C U J C R E T A U T B
S M N K E U S U T S H S
U E I C H Y I R E Y G S
B I K L O N W L R R I E
E M A A L H I O F R R N
I A T R L C H U I A W K
N J A A O N C G E H A R
A O R O W M O H L A R A
L G I S A S A S D E A H
E R N W Y A L N K W B K
M A A A Y S I A C R C
G N N L O R E C O I A A
N T C D I D E N C E B J
```

Never ignore coincidence. Unless, of course, you're busy, in which case, always ignore coincidence.

50. WORDS TO MAKE YOU SOUND SMART

```
M Y R C H A R I S M A M
A N H A E C A N A P E T
R A E C L T S Y R T M I
E S T I G R N T V E O A
D L O L O C S A L F T E
A I R L D I R U L K I L
L Z I Y H S I V E S P G
O E C D T Y A O T E E G
C U R I E F G N T O M O
C I N U O G A A G A A D
A P T N O T C W U S N N
M F R N T O S D H A T O
A U R E V E L E I L R O
R B L I C I D A L L A B
A I U A N O T H E T A I
D O N M N E C A N R E D
E U A I C T C I O E V P
R I S T R B I Q O I A T
I T M A I V U D R U U K
E O B L Z E A L O U S U
E U G O R B R N N T E T
T S I S S I C R A N E T
```

My mantra is: Realize you're going to fail all the time, and accept it. —Mark Burnett

51. EPONYMS A-K

```
J O U L E L Y O B W H E
N Y H E I N E K E N B O
S E L L I H C A C U O J
H C I L M I E H K W Y A
A A A N U O R S E T C C
F S L B D T R A O R O U
O A Z F E E O T R B T Z
F N H O L L W F S R T Z
O O E R L L L E O G E I
R V I L E T H E Y R N F
B A M S W N C O R A D A
E R E P M A H H L H O T
S I R D T O E E N A L K
D E I W O B V R I M B I
B C E V U L R S V T Y N
E L E N T A O H L H E S
R R S S G H L E E T R U
I E U P S O E Y K T H I
N O A T T N T L O C O S
G L O C K D A V O N B L
T R O F U A E B I S M E
A R C K R E L S Y R H C
```

When you want to fool the world, tell the truth.
—Otto von Bismarck

52. EPONYMS L-W

```
I D L E N P A R H S O N
P T A S T R A U S S C A
E H C S R O P R E T H A
N T S E M A C H T H E E
N Y A T S S E D T O L S
E L P T E M L S Y P I R
Y D E E E A V A M I E O
C U N U N O B E L G W M
R A R O O E T E N A T H
A T D H S T W I T N H K
E C Y L A N S T D O N
M T T I M H I L O B A V
I U O S A X T K U N E D
L A R E U T E R R T R N
Q Y B P R O L F O A Z T
U S L H H E T I T O P R
E A E O E Y S O W O A N
T L D N N G E I N K V O
O C N L O L N Z A T L E
A H A O G N I R U T O S
S O M E L B A T L O V L
T W I N C H E S T E R A
```

I don't care that they stole my idea.
I care that they don't have any of their own.
—Nikola Tesla

53. GEOLOGY WHIZ

I went into geology because I like being
outdoors, and because everybody ... seemed
like free spirits or renegades or something.

54. STATE MOTTOS

This became a credo of mine ... attempt the
impossible in order to improve your work.
—Bette Davis

55. I'M NUMBER ONE: 2000s

Whether I'm wearing lots of makeup or no
makeup, I'm always the same person inside.

56. STEPHEN KING CHARACTERS

You cannot hope to sweep someone
else away by the force of your
writing until it has been done to you.

57. HAPPY EARTH DAY

```
M I D D L E E A S T F O
A R G S E T D E N L O T
I T I H A E D T T E A H
L X E E G I A R T V C H
A N O R T H P O L E I P
R R E D U T I T A L R R
T E C I T N A L T A E I
S O U T H P O L E E M M
U O D E I L I G H S A E
A T U P A C I F I C L M
S C T T O F E A I S A E
E L I Y H O U R B E R R
A R E R F A E E R T T I
A N L D E T M E H E N D
X W I O N M H E D S E I
L O O N N P A F R I C A
G T N O S G P H O I L N
A N A I D N I Y T W C I
T H M Y U O U T A R R A
H E A I R Q K A U H O L
H E P O R U E I Q D L N
G I B R O Z O N E A E N
```

Forget not that the earth delights to feel your bare feet and the winds long to play with your hair. —Kahlil Gibran

58. ROM-COMS

```
T A H T L L A S E H S P
T H E C I L A T T W R I
H I N G T L G E A E B L
O U H T L I R G T D O L
M T A Y R H S T N D P O
S C R M A E Y I G I U W
E I A U B W A S N N K S
T P E O O P D A I G A L
A N V M U F E D P E E O
D A A N T L N O E Y R R
T N L W L G I O E N B U
S N E E A T F G L E K N
R I N T S O E S S W C A
I E T G T T N A E Y U W
F H I T N C O R N E R A
H A N E I R R R I A T Y
G L E H G T A T Y R S T
H L S E H V E R Y S N E
N D D M T L O V E E O A
T S A F K A E R B V O C
T I Y T H G I M U E M A
O R A C N E E R G L L Y
```

The thing about romance is people only get together right at the very end. —"Love Actually"

59. TIME'S MOST INFLUENTIAL MEN (2014)

```
E I R D D A K L A N J O
Y T M C M A S T E R Z H
R F R A N C I S O E O E
I R Y B E Z O S P J B O
A A H M D U E O R N A E
L H C C W I L L I A M S
C M T C O R U D A M A D
N A A O N K E Y E O Z A
I N B N S E O Y O D N N
S F R A L J E V E I A G
C I E U F R E U A T L O
U H B G S I J N Q C S T
A O M H A W I W N C D E
R L U E N A N O O T M N
O D C Y W L P R J U K A
N E O R A E I B S T C D
A R L R L G N H A C I L
L C L E K E G R E E N A
D T I K E I S I S L A H
O H N J R P F A D E L L
E E S N U S H E R M A N
Y H P R U M D G A M K E
```

Enjoy the journey of life and not just the endgame.

60. TIME'S MOST INFLUENTIAL WOMEN (2014)

```
W H B E Y O N C E P E H
T A Y L O R N A H N N A
T T H D E I W I H O H Y
B O R N T L L E S O O H
A B R A M O V I C U K O
R W M R T O L R S N O E
R D L B D L I A U D N C
A Y W I E S F N L E J Y
D W E L S Z I D I R O R
A H R L A L C E S W I U
M I G I L E L R T O W S
S T I G G E I S Y O E N
N E T T E H N O A D A R
W A T E R S T N N V L U
P E E B N O O L I N A B
A E P A V O N O N M L I
U C E C B E K P G E T C
L O M H K O E E S R H S
U P O E L W E Z I K A C
S U L L I V A N H E N R
F L O E S M A I L L I W
Y H U T E N E S S A M L
```

When the whole world is silent, even one voice becomes powerful.

61. STUDY HAUL

Basic research is what I am doing when I don't know what I am doing.

62. MY LITTLE PONY

I like funny words! One of my favorite funny words is "kumquat!"

63. 5-LETTER SCRABBLE WORDS

Playing bop is like playing Scrabble with all the vowels missing.

64. 6-LETTER SCRABBLE WORDS

Children are the most desirable opponents at Scrabble as they are both easy to beat and fun to cheat.

65. I'M NUMBER ONE: 2010s

Trust is hard to come by. That's why my circle is small and tight. I'm kind of funny about making new friends.

66. WE ARE STAR STUFF

Keep your eyes on the stars, but remember to keep your feet on the ground.
—Theodore Roosevelt

67. "STAR WARS"

The Force is what gives a Jedi his power. It's an energy field created by all living things.

68. PRESIDENTIAL MEDAL OF FREEDOM IN THE ARTS

To create one's own world in any of the arts takes courage.

69. DICKENS CHARACTERS

```
T H E P F L D F C A I L
Y N K O O R K F H O G I
C F P W A S E U A A I L
N R T Z I K T D R G W I
A E Z K I B A I L N I A
N A R M E M R D E G Z N
B A S L S I T L Y G Z I
B S L T Y Y F E B R E C
A E O N D O U I A A F H
R O T D N T L F T I R O
T E I S E H D R E N M L
T B N I Y N O E S G R A
I S G Y C T D P O E B S
N T I T A U G P H R R N
Y A E W R P E O S E O I
T G J D T O R C R M W C
I G L K O R R D E I N K
M E Y E N O E I Z T L L
S O F N O M E V T T O E
E T H G U H I A I I W B
N G E E A G A D B L I Y
N N I F F O B Y D D O N
```

The pain of parting is nothing
to the joy of meeting again.

70. BATMAN TV SOUND EFFECTS

```
K L E A I I E E H W O
L T S G O E R Q I C H O
O O B I E N U W W N A O
N Y R I K N G E O U C O
K N A L C N V E Z R K F
T S K K A E T M P C K F
T A K B A B N P A O R F
O K K S A T P A W P U I
L O O M R U R P O O L B
Z C A U R R P A Y S H L
K Z E G C O R H E P Y U
S N Z B L H O W E L U R
T L O Z H S Z P E A O P
N F O R Z I A W H A M M
F T B S V W P S H T K E
R O A O H S A D S N T O
A B R T N R I C O W W W
T H W A C K L L P A B I
G H T L N O Z O A I E H
R T U U O O M P A O L G
R N H S R P P A W H T G
K T H C N U R K S O W U
```

Let's go, Robin. We've set another youth
on the road to a brighter tomorrow.

71. SONDHEIM SONGS

```
S A W T I E K I L A R P
T L U A F R U O Y T I R
E E N Y N A H P I P E E
P L O V I N G Y O U W T
M P O O R B A B Y I H T
U O T V S D E H L F I Y
R E B M E M E R O A S L
T P I S A L N W J T A
N D A E R I Y A R T L D
E E T A H M I S S R E Y
M R H N E D T N E L A E
O D G O V O W M P D S M
M N I L I O P M N N I I
Y U N E L G I U O G R T
N H O C A S S S L N A R
A R T R G T I T I I P U
T E Y A N A O M F H H O
B H D B I H R O E T A A
I T E L E T N R G R G O
R O M D B D E E E O R O
U N O W Y O U K N O W T
O A C F C G H Y A P O S
```

Art, in itself, is an attempt
to bring order out of chaos.

72. "GAME OF THRONES"

```
S A M W E L L T A R L Y
A F W I D D H E N Y O L
N M U N D P M L A Y T L
S O H T A E M U M G A U
A N R E R R M Y R A R T
B B O R D E B O C E C R
R E B F S R O D N A S E
O N E E T F T L T R H T
N J R L A H Y E R Y O S
N E T L R N L R K A O O
Y N B E K Y Y E H V S H
R Y A C N T O U A S E W
R M R Y E I T A L T M N
A F A P O R R Y D H I Y
N L T R O B S U R G A D
O O H Y G I Y E O I J S
J W E T W A R H G W O I
E E O E R I E E O I F N
O R N S N O N R M I F N
R I C K O N E D Y D R A
L D T H E W A L L E E T
G R O U N D D V A R Y S
```

When you play the game of thrones, you
win or you die. There is no middle ground.

73. SERIF FONTS

I do not think of type as something that should be readable. It should be beautiful.
—Ed Benguiat

74. SANS-SERIF FONTS

Typography is the craft of endowing human language with a durable visual form.
—Robert Bringhurst

75. DON'T PANIC

A towel ... is about the most massively useful thing an interstellar hitchhiker can have.

76. TALK LIKE AN EGYPTIAN

What I'm dealing with is so vast and great that it can't be called the truth. It's above the truth. —Sun Ra

77. POLISH CITIES

```
M O S G T P E O L P L E
A S K D F O R H U A P P
I N E Y K L Z A B R Z E
S S O N N A E C L O N C
N E C I W I L G I D I I
I K R A K O W I N T I W
L O N H A E Z K S I P O
A W O H C O T S E Z C T
Z P A L I T N N E E H A
S S E L O D Z A N Z O K
O I S R B C A D I K R N
K O U A N R P G C L Z Y
E N B D A O Z O E E O F
W E L O T W L Y Z I W F
A Y O M W P A S C N U D
L O N M R T S Z Z H A E
C E I W O N S O S T T N
O L A P C T N Y A R Y C
L B O O L N Y R D H A N
W L I T A I N B C O N W
E A A R W O T Y H U R R
U G B I W N T S T E I N
```

Most people ask for happiness on condition. Happiness can only be felt if you don't set any condition. —Arthur Rubinstein

78. RULERS OF JAPAN

```
M U Y G G R O A N O D F
A M T H E Z E R W Y A U
N N S A N A Z A K M M D
E E S E M S C E I N N N
D T K U E A N T A I I O
F T K N I H E K T N J E
A A O M I Z O I I P U E
R W N A N N E I E O S R
A A I N O Z N I K J U D
O K N E I W K U Y I Z E
Y A S E S W S O J M A J
G R H E R T M A B M K I
N I O E E E O B V U U N
I H M R I E K O S K N G
E S U S H U N T O R Y U
M B R N O W A Y E A K U
N L A N R D G T H O K H
I O K N I O O Y T O O C
K Y A B K N J N K T G I
O A M K A A I E Z I E R
O D I O W N U N U N J N O
J U N N A K N E S A G A
```

My grandfather was a descendant of the Emperor and we were very wealthy. —Yoko Ono

79. IT TAKES TWO

```
G H A R D Y O O D N G I
G C A C S H Y N O T N A
T E G N L O O O E T O M
D C N I S A N N G O H L
H H T P A E R N R B C E
T C L Y D E L K Y B I H
N G O I V A S E T A O T
S S L A U U L N N E P C
H S L R R R W I E E E T
S O E R I E A Y R L O W
T L T H H T H K A L T J
I E S S P J A C K I H U
A K O A I L L O L N S L
A N C L S Y L R G N O I
B U L L W I N K L E O E
E F E D N B M I L T I T
R R O G O E M O R N G E
T A P G H S U T N R I L
T G A I L I L O E I N L
T R T B S W B T E M G E
T F R E D E E R N I E R
O B A C A L L R R O R W
```

Good night, good night! Parting is such sweet sorrow, that I shall say good night till it be morrow.

80. WORD SANDWICHES

```
I C M N O T N A S A I N
D W H I C Y H E S T S O
R E K A D I E U E T A H
A T N L N O N L Y L W S
E L O L S G G N I G A T
U M W E S T E R N R N B
B K N E Y S T S E O A P
N U D W O I A C R E R H
E S R H I R B P S E D E
L L C N A A A L S E O Y
T C A C T I B T B O F D
I F F L H E O O I R W M
E I V I E D L N A O I T
T H I M M G T H O R N Y
T N G A E S G S K L D A
S F D X E Y E Y K L I M
E L G D L A T T I C E W
X O I A L A C R O S S E
A W H I R L M H A M T L
L E D U C A T E I P E S
C R A N K Y L G N D A H
H Y E N A P A C U T E A
```

I'm not a sandwich store that only sells turkey sandwiches. I sell a lot of different things. —Lady Gaga

WORD LISTS

79. IT TAKES TWO
ABBOTT & COSTELLO
ANTONY & CLEOPATRA
BERT & ERNIE
BOGART & BACALL
BONNIE & CLYDE
CAPTAIN & TENNILLE
CHEECH & CHONG
FRED & GINGER
HALL & OATES
HANSEL & GRETEL
JACK & JILL
LAUREL & HARDY
LAVERNE & SHIRLEY
LEWIS & CLARK
PENN & TELLER
ROCKY & BULLWINKLE
ROMEO & JULIET
SIMON & GARFUNKEL
SONNY & CHER
THELMA & LOUISE

WORD LISTS

80. WORD SANDWICHES

ABATE
ABOARD
ACUTE
ADIEU
AGING
APART
APRON
AWASH
AWHIRL
BALEEN
BURNT
CACTI
CHANGE
CHIDE
CHOSEN
CLIMAX
CRANKY
EDUCATE
EMOTE
FLOWERY
GLOBE

GREEDY
HYENA
IVIED
KNOWN
LACROSSE
LAMENT
LATTICE
LAXEST
LEGGY
MILKY
MIRKY
MOLDY
ORATION
PLEASE
PRESTO
THEME
THORNY
WELSH
WESTERN
WIDEST
WINDIEST

About the Author

PATRICK BLINDAUER has published puzzles in places like The New York Times, The Wall Street Journal, and The Washington Post. His other books include "Absolutely Nasty Word Search, Level Three," "Easy Breezy Crosswords," "Easy Like Monday Morning Crosswords," and "Large Print Sudoku."

Blindauer was born on the Fourth of July and grew up mostly in North Dakota. He studied theater in college, moved to New York City in 1998, and had a few successes in acting (including appearing in seven episodes of a show called "Strangers With Candy" and having a line in the film "A Beautiful Mind").

His first puzzle was published in The New York Times on July 21, 2005 (a Thursday). He has since written over 60 puzzles for the paper, including a week-long crossword contest. He also writes puzzles as a freelancer for the American Values Club Crossword, is a frequent contributor to the American Crossword Puzzle Tournament, and cohosts an annual crossword tournament, Lollapuzzoola, in New York City.

In his spare time, Blindauer enjoys letterboxing with his wife, Rebecca, or playing frisbee with his dog-ter, Penny. He lives in St. Louis, and his website address is www.patrickblindauer.com.